Life Talks
THE CONVERSATIONS CONTINUE

By Peggy Jennings-Severe

This book is dedicated to my mother, Patricia Ann Dickinson Jennings, and to my daughter, Ana Laura Severe-Karatekeli—two of my greatest teachers.

May this book honor my mother's legacy, further develop my own, and introduce my daughter to hers.

Photo taken circa 2000

Mom

You ushered me in,
I escorted you out.

You cried with joy,
I cried with pain.

You held me tight,
I let you go.

You sang and soothed,
So did I.

You let me go,
I hung on.

You knew it was my time,
I knew it was yours.

You loved my babies,
I've learned to love yours.

You lost count of your blessings,
I lost count of the doses.

Your breathing slowed down,
Mine sped up.

You ushered me in,
I escorted you out.

Written by Peggy Jennings-Severe, 2004

TABLE OF CONTENTS

I believe that each of us has relationships—with our children, our spouse, our relatives, our friends, our neighbors, and our colleagues—that we want to enjoy, deepen, and enrich.

I believe that each of us longs to have our interactions with others—especially those we treasure and value—to be meaningful.

I believe that each of us has an inherent desire to belong.

I believe that Life Talks—A Guide to Bringing Back Conversation and now Life Talks—The Conversations Continue provide the tools to accomplish all three!

Peggy Jennings-Severe, June 2015

INTRODUCTION

It took me many years to realize how unique and special my relationship with my mother was and how much I listened and benefitted from her wisdom growing up. I thought all mothers told their daughters deep and intimate things about life and relationships and how difficult and rewarding both can be. But in talking with other women, I have come to realize how unusual our relationship was and how lucky I was to be Patricia Ann Dickinson Jennings's daughter.
One thing I was aware of early in my adolescence and young adulthood is that women gravitated to my mother. In her, they found someone who was safe and easy to confide in. They would often come to our home, sit in the kitchen, drink coffee, and in hushed tones share their worries and concerns with her. Some of their burdens were so personal that even their husbands were unaware of them. They sought out her advice because she was kind (without being a pushover), comfortable in her own skin, and slow to judge. But most importantly they came to my mother because she could keep a secret.

These women's secrets quickly became my lessons, and I proved to be a willing and eager student of life under my mother's tutelage. It helped that I was innately curious (some would say nosy) about people, sensitive (maybe too sensitive, my mother would say), and I too could keep confidences when the situation called for it.

I must have been a good listener too, because here it is over ten years since my mother's passing, and I still find myself sharing my mother's stories, wisdom, and insights with anyone who is willing to listen—my children, my students, my friends, and now my readers. Those closest to me are probably tired of hearing me say, "My mother used to say..." But heck, if it's good advice, it's good advice. And good advice, like a compass, often helps you figure out where you are and what direction you need to go. Many women left my mother's kitchen a little less lost and a lot more loved.

Of all the advice she gave me, one piece in particular has had a lasting impact. "Peggy," she told me, "words are powerful and not to be used lightly, because once they are spoken you can never take them back." She illustrated her point by telling me about a fight our neighbors Mr. and Mrs. North had had recently. Apparently, Mrs. North told her husband, in a fit of anger mixed with alcohol, that he was an inadequate lover. Being a young teen at the time, I didn't fully understand the complexities of this insult, but I was smart enough to know that her criticism was harsh, highly insensitive, and hit Mr. North "below the belt." My mom went on to advise me that no matter how much Mrs. North apologized or repented the next day, her husband would always be left with doubt regarding his masculinity and attractiveness. Not surprisingly, the Norths divorced several years later and I never forgot my mother's sound and prophetic advice.

To be fair, my father mentored me as well but more indirectly. I learned my father's lessons by observing him while keeping a safe distance away from his high expectations and unpredictable temper. Nevertheless, he and my mother were both extremely curious people, avid readers of newspapers, magazines, and books, and they shared a love for travel. They especially enjoyed engaging in—you guessed it—stimulating conversations with others no matter what age or educational attainment the speaker may have acquired. As long as you weren't ignorant or arrogant, my father was interested in you and what you thought about things. My young high school and college friends were both honored and mortified that he wanted to know what they thought about the upcoming elections, Washington Husky football, and their future—all in one conversation. Asking questions was nearly as natural as breathing in my family. We were taught that questions were the way you showed another person your interest and respect.

What my mother and father didn't teach me—at least directly—is that the absence of words is equally significant in the world of relationships. This I learned on my own.

Raised in a home and an era where fathers' focus was often on their careers and their sons, I longed, as the only daughter and the baby of the family, to hear words of acknowledgment, encouragement, and interest from my father. Ironically, my father sought out and listened to other people's opinions and ideas but only rarely his own daughter's. As a result, we were often left with little to say to each other.

I also remember vividly and somewhat painfully a time, years ago, when

I was working full time outside the home and a mother to two toddlers, that my conversations with my husband became fewer and less meaningful at the end of each exhausting day. If we weren't discussing tomorrow's logistics, such as who was taking Ben to the doctor or picking up Annie from day care, we weren't talking. Instead we escaped life's pressures by getting lost in a book or a TV show. It took counseling and commitment to turn this bad habit and our marriage around. Looking back, then, it is not surprising, given my mother's people skills, my father's curious nature, and my observational skills and yearning to connect with others, that I should write a book designed to promote meaningful conversations and strengthen relationships. But it was not until graduate school that I found the tool I was looking for to accomplish this: open-ended questions!

Why Open-Ended Questions?

Who is God? Who am I? How can I support you? Who cares? How do I feel about that? What belief am I willing to die for? What brings me joy? What is my purpose? Why? Why not? Like words, questions can be powerful too. Granted, some questions aren't questions at all, but are just expressions of our emotions or reactions to an event: "What the hell?" "Who died and made you the boss?" And my favorite, "Really?" (said with lots of sarcasm and your head tilted at an angle). These questions don't require an answer at all. Instead they allow us to blow off some steam or buy us some time so that we can gain a clearer picture as to what we really think or feel about a situation.

We also use questions to gain clarity. "Huh?" "Who said so?" "How can I help you?" and "How do you want me to do that?" are some examples.

Personally, I have a habit—and my family would tell you it is a bad one—of using questions as a way to direct others to do something for me. For instance, I will often say to my family, "Did you notice the dishes were still dirty?" or "Would you mind cleaning the dishes?" when I really mean "Clean the dishes and do it now!" Oops.

The questions that I find to be the most powerful, though, and the type that this book uses are the open-ended kind that encourage us to explore more deeply, with ourselves or others, our ideas and feelings and hear them out loud—exposing them to the light of day, so to speak.

I learned about the power of words from my mother, but I learned the power of questions from a psychology professor I had in graduate school. My goal when I first started graduate school was to become a counselor either in a high school setting or in private practice somewhere. One of the first courses I enrolled in was titled "Individual Counseling" (versus group or family counseling) and was taught by a newly hired and comparatively young (under fifty) professor. He was refreshing to me because he did not totally buy into the scripted model of counseling called "active listening" that was en vogue at the time and championed by the Psychology Department's old guard. Active listening essentially required the counselor to reflect back—or parrot, as we called it then—what the client had just said. There were stages associated with the active listening model and recommended phrases to say at each step.

I hated it. I felt like a robot—though a compassionate one—and way too hemmed in by what I thought was a one-size-fits-all approach. Luckily, my professor was a bit of a renegade (he didn't last long at this university) and deviated from the revered model to the ire of the older, more established faculty. When I complained to him (as only a self-righteous and know-it-all graduate student can) about how artificial and uninspiring the active listening approach was, he quietly suggested, "Why don't you use open-ended questions to help your clients explore their thoughts and feelings?"

Hallelujah! I had found the Promised Land, and it worked like a charm. No longer was I focused on trying to remember the required response, but instead I was able to actually listen more deeply and give the client my undivided attention and feel more authentic to boot! This approach felt much more natural to me and proved to be very effective not just with clients first and students later, but in my personal life as well.

Who knew that over thirty years later, I would write a book about the power of questions? Thanks, Mom, Dad, and Professor R.!

Why Traditions?

Now that we have identified one essential ingredient, open-ended questions, for a quality conversation, how do we use them? Do we just spring them on our children, friends, and loved ones without warning? Take our chances and see what happens? The answer is yes and no. Open-ended questions can stand alone. You can ask a question to yourself or to others, taking turns or not following any particular pattern at all. Or you can insert your well-thought-out questions in an activity. If the activity is repeated or associated with a special event or holiday, it can morph into a tradition!

I don't think I am a traditionalist in the strictest sense. I like change too much, and I am impervious to the argument that we should do something again and again simply because we have always done it that way. Nevertheless, I sure do value and appreciate traditions and am convinced of their value.

Nearly fifteen years ago, a colleague of mine and I organized a Working

Parents Support Group that met monthly on our college campus. The idea behind the group was to meet regularly to discuss and support each other as we traversed and muddled through the unique and sometimes overwhelming challenges of working full time and parenting full time. I don't remember much about what was discussed during our meetings, but I do remember that we decided early in the group's formation to disallow complaining and whining. This rule wasn't always easy for us to maintain, but it did keep us on track and more likely to discuss the meatier issues such as glass ceilings and parental guilt.

One discussion I remember vividly, though, and it has stayed with me to this day. It was related to traditions and their importance in the building of healthy and secure children and families. All of the members of our support group were women and worked in either Student Services or were faculty who taught in the Social Sciences and Human Development departments. So we were a pretty homogeneous bunch and tended to think alike. Thus, it may not be surprising that we all agreed that children, and parents for that matter, needed traditions. What I took away from this conversation and have believed ever since is this: we humans have a fundamental need, which is probably linked to our very survival, to have stable, ongoing, and meaningful connections with others. Others may include family, friends, neighbors, schoolmates, social groups, athletic teams, church members, and so forth. And it is traditions that often insure that people establish and maintain these vital and life-sustaining connections in a regular and predictable way. The Merriam-Webster dictionary defines a tradition as "an inherited, established, or customary pattern of thought, action, or behavior." Even our Working Parents Support Group ultimately met this definition.

But I also realize that traditions alone are not enough. In fact I think many of us approach and plan traditions in an "autopilot" manner. For instance, if it is Thanksgiving, we often invite the same mandatory relatives and friends, we eat the same food, watch the same football games, and complain about our same old expanding waist lines, then go home knowing we will repeat this holiday in the same way next year. No mystery. No surprises. No fun.

What I just described is indeed a stable and predictable tradition, but it lacked one important ingredient: meaning. I wrote about this common experience in an article for North State Parent magazine (see page 103). Our intent is always good. No one wants to plan a less-than-fulfilling event. What we lack sometimes is imagination and ideas. What is missing is a set of questions or an activity that will provide an opportunity for those participating in these important traditions to learn something new about each other that will spark further conversation or create a commonality or link that didn't exist before.

Now that I have argued on behalf of traditions, you might find it odd that I feel it necessary to add a disclaimer or word of caution. As an avid reader of spiritual self-help books, but finisher of few, I often find myself rebelling and tossing aside these types of books when I sense the author is beginning to chastise me for leading my life in the wrong manner. I really bristle when he or she suggests that he or she has the answer that will magically fit for not just me but everyone! It's that one-size-fits-all approach that doesn't ring true for me.

I come from a long line of independent thinkers, and my father always warned us children about "black-and-white thinking." So though I am a strong proponent of building and sustaining positive and community-building traditions, I also want to state—just as strongly—that there is no "one right way." This awareness has taken me a while to fully embrace. But I have learned this by observing and talking with many people whom I know, respect, and love well (some are my own family members and coworkers) and who sincerely don't have a need for reoccurring traditions—religious or otherwise. They are usually willing to participate when others initiate, but are just as happy not. In our zeal to create connections, let's make sure we don't isolate or ostracize those who are just as happy observing or walking away from them. We need to make room for their self-expression and choices as well.

Having said that, however, I have also witnessed naysayers come around too. Both in my family and at work, I have watched people who initially or periodically chose not to participate in my wonderful team builders, only to have them join or rejoin at the next opportunity. So, as my mother used to say, always keep the door open. Give people space, but at the same time continue to find ways to close the gap. The following questions and traditions are designed to do just that!

How Do I Start?
Recommendations for Success

Many, though not all, of the questions and activities that I have included in this book are ones that I have used personally and more than once. I have learned through trial and error what works and doesn't work, at least from my perspective. So avoid my mistakes, and consider these recommendations before you initiate your first guided conversation or community-building activity.

1. Be considerate. Prepare your participants, especially those that are young, introverted, or generally resistant to structured games or activities. Whenever

possible, let people know in advance (an hour or more) what the activity is going to be and their specific role in it. The first person I shared my list of anniversary questions with was a coworker of mine, who after reading over the set of questions, said, "Oh my, I had better e-mail these to my husband even before we leave for Hawaii to celebrate our anniversary." Her introverted husband needed time to think about his answers without the pressure of his wife staring at him from across the restaurant table.

2. Be spontaneous. You are not required to use the book literally, using the questions only during the designated event (chapter). Mix and match and improvise. Two summers ago, my husband's relatives—all of them, and some of their friends too—came to our "happy place" in Oregon for the Annual Severe Family Reunion. Typically the reunion lasts no more than a week, but that year, because of where the Fourth of July landed, the reunion stretched to nine long days. Even the most functional families would have a hard time surviving that long together, especially when confined to one acre. As you might suspect, a conflict arose and there became a chill in the air that no warm summer day could thaw. I decided something needed to be done and announced to the group that that evening around the campfire, each person, young and old, would share his or her personal highlight of the reunion. Almost immediately, the atmosphere shifted. People began to concentrate on all the fun and joy they had experienced instead of the one argument that now seemed inconsequential in comparison.

3. Be creative. A coworker of mine bought a copy of Life Talks for her two adult daughters. One daughter was in her midtwenties, married, and had two young sons. She contacted me shortly after she received and read the book and was eager to tell me how she and her husband had used the questions. Together, they took turns answering random questions from the book over the phone each night. He worked and lived out of town six days a week, and she was excited to have a way to maintain a sense of intimacy with him during the long week of separation. They used the contents of Life Talks in a totally unforeseen and creative way. Please feel free to do the same.

4. Be courageous. My daughter, Annie, and I met a woman at a farmers' market in Oregon. She purchased Life Talks hoping to reconnect with her adult sons, who had distanced themselves from her after her rather nasty divorce from their father. One of her sons had a birthday that was soon approaching, and she felt that some of the questions from the book would serve as a starting point for her to begin to

bridge the gulf she felt lay between them.

5. Be positive and non-judgmental. Accept the answers to the questions and the conversation that ensues as a gift. The quickest way to insure that no one will want to participate again in your team builder is to respond or interpret his or her answers in a negative way or imply that his or her answer was wrong or inadequate. To answer some of the questions in this book will be risky for many, and if they suspect that they are being judged or evaluated, you can be assured that they will avoid—at all costs—your next initiative.

6. Prompting the young is OK. One of the things I think is most powerful about these conversation-based traditions is that they prepare and provide children with the opportunity to develop and share a language and vocabulary of love, friendship, gratitude, and feelings in general. We included our grandson Aydin in some of these activities starting at the age of two. For instance, we started by asking Aydin what he appreciated about his father on Father's Day. Aydin talks nonstop ordinarily, but this stumped him, so we asked, "Do you like that he plays with you?" "Do you like that he reads to you and tucks you in at night?" Each time he said yes and repeated the statement. Aydin was and is learning to share his love and appreciation verbally, and that is a skill we can't learn too early.

AM I/ARE WE READY TO COMMIT/GET MARRIED?

I met my husband early. I was seventeen and he was sixteen. My parents liked Rhys from the start, but as we became serious a year or so later, they let their concerns and worries be known. They didn't discourage us outright when we told them of our plans to marry, but my mother in particular would ask me some pretty pointed questions—many of which I had trouble answering. My father, on the other hand, just kept asking me one question: – "Which college are you going to transfer to and when?" He chose to ignore the marriage option altogether.

Around this same time, I began taking classes at my local community college. During my first semester, I enrolled in a course titled "Self-Awareness." Before you snicker, remember that this was the '70s—1974, to be exact. The only section of "Self-Awareness" still open when I registered was the one scheduled at night. This was fortuitous.

On the first night the class was held, I had trouble finding the classroom. It was located in the basement of the library. When I first walked in, I noticed immediately that there were no desks nor chairs—just pillows on the floor. I looked around at the other students and quickly realized that I was probably the youngest person in the room. Most of the students were women in their late twenties or early thirties and were returning to school after a significant break. And once the class got rolling, I learned that many had done what I had planned to do: gotten married right out of high school. Looking back, most of these ladies said they would have done things differently. Most were now divorced. Many were now single parents.

I learned a lot from these women. They challenged my thinking and assumptions about marriage and asked me many difficult questions. When my answers seemed naïve or not well thought out, they let me know it. And if I wasn't able to answer at all, they concluded, and rightfully so, that I wasn't ready to get married!

Fortunately, I took my parents' and my fellow students' advice and waited until I was more mature and experienced enough to be able to answer some of their questions. As it turned out, my "self-awareness" didn't happen overnight. Rhys and I got married six years later.

Though I can't remember specifically what my mother and my classmates asked me decades ago, I suspect their influence is reflected in the questions below. Answer them individually, or better yet, together with your partner. Hopefully these questions will help you make one of the most important decisions of your life: to commit or not to commit.

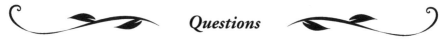

Questions

1. Are you both better people because you are in a relationship together? *(This is one of my favorite questions.)*
2. Do you bring out and reinforce the best in each other? How?
3. Do you share the same values? What are they?
4. Does your partner have good and close friends?
5. How does your partner treat women and men?
6. How does your partner treat his or her family?
7. How does his or her family treat you?
8. How does your partner treat those who have little power or influence?
9. Is your partner willing to seek help *(therapy, couples retreat, religious-based counseling, etc.)* when and if an issue(s) arises that you cannot successfully resolve?
10. Can you live with the idiosyncrasies and flaws that you perceive in your partner? *(My mother often said that you marry your partner not only because of his or her personal strengths and attributes, but more importantly because you can live with his or her faults as well.)*
11. Can you apologize to your partner when you are at fault?
12. Can your partner apologize to you when he or she is at fault?
13. Can you make each other laugh?
14. Do you respect each other? How is it demonstrated?
15. Is your partner interesting to you?
16. Do you have common interests?

17. Do you have separate interests?
18. Does your world expand or contract as a result of being a couple?
19. Are you physically and sexually attracted to each other?
20. Can you both express what you need and want sexually?
21. Are you both comfortable with your own bodies?
22. Are you both willing to bring up issues about the relationship and in a timely way?
23. Are you both aware of the baggage you bring from your family of origin?
24. Are you willing to grow and change as a person and couple, and are you willing to allow that in the other?
25. Do you have good role models for healthy relationships?
26. Do you both have relationship stamina? Can you go the distance?
27. Do you both have realistic expectations about long-term relationships?
28. Are you comfortable being vulnerable and accepting support from your partner?
29. Are you comfortable providing support to your partner when he or she is feeling vulnerable?
30. Are you willing to put your needs aside (on occasion) and put your partner's needs first?

AM I/ARE WE READY TO BE PARENTS?

After our children were born, I understood something in a new and profound way. I understood why people choose not to have them. Oops. Did I say that out loud? Before you call my children and commiserate with them for having such a horrible mother, let me state that I also, simultaneously, understood in a totally unimaginable and awe-inspiring way, why people wanted so badly to be parents. I fully get, understand, and support both decisions. Children change your life—in good and not-so-good ways—like nothing else can or will. And the decision to have them should not be entered into lightly.

Ideally, babies—as well as the two-year-olds and teens they turn into—deserve to be born to parents who have weighed, as best they could, the pros and cons of parenthood. In an ideal world, children would come into this world invited by one or more adults who took the time to consider and then intentionally chose to be a parent.

I recognize that this is a rather ambitious dream and "surprises" often happen. According to one source for instance, nearly 40 percent of births in the United States are the result of unintended pregnancies. As a matter of fact, my husband was an unanticipated gift, and I doubt his parents had the opportunity, time, or inclination to answer many, if any, of the questions below. But it was also a different time and generation.

In some ways, I think people who choose to adopt have an advantage in this regard, as they are required as part of the process of adoption to spend copious amounts of time completing paperwork, participating in interviews, and undergoing home inspections. It is truly parenthood by choice with a lot of deliberation and soul searching involved. Because I have quite a few adopted members in my family, including nieces, nephew, and cousins, I have asked some of them to contribute to the section of questions below that might be unique to the process of adoption. Thank you, Emilie and Pat!

Regardless of which way you bring children into your life, if you do at all, I wish you the gift of time for contemplation and reflection before, during, and after conception or adoption. I hope that the questions contained in this chapter will help you gain the clarity you need to help you make (or accept) what is likely to be one of the biggest and most impactful decisions of your life!

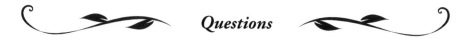

Questions

Should I/We Become Parents?

1. Why do you want to be a parent? *(Always a good place to start.)*
2. What do you expect from parenthood?
3. Are you expecting parenthood to fill a void? If so, in what ways? What if it doesn't?
4. Are you healthy enough mentally and physically to become pregnant and be a parent?
5. Are you ready and willing to experience the changes, good and not so good, that your body will experience while pregnant?
6. What skills or traits do you currently possess that will make you a good parent?
7. What skills or traits do you currently lack that will be necessary to be a good parent?
8. What resources *(financial, space, medical, knowledge, etc.)* do you have available to allow or assist you to be a good parent?
9. Do you have an adequate support system to help and mentor you as you parent?
10. How would you feel and what would you do if the fetus or baby is not the gender you hoped for?
11. How would you feel and what would you do if the fetus or baby had significant medical or developmental problems?
12. Is your current and future lifestyle flexible enough to include a child?
13. In what ways are you willing to modify your life to accommodate a child?
14. In what ways are you not willing to modify your life to accommodate a child?
15. If sharing parenting responsibilities, are you both clear as to your role expectations and task distribution?

(I think this is a very important question for a couple to discuss. I have often spoken to women who were disappointed with their male partners for not being more involved and responsible for child rearing. Likewise, I have met a lot of women who say they want help from their partners but thwart or undermine the father's help to the point where the father stops trying. Either situation often creates tension and additional stress on the relationship.)

16. How much is family or peer pressure impacting your decision regarding parenthood?
17. If a couple, do you agree in terms of discipline, religious upbringing, and overall parenting style?
18. If you choose not to become a parent, how will you address the disappointment that family and friends may experience?
19. What if you have difficulty conceiving? What are you willing to do at that point?

Adoption-Specific Questions

1. Have you made peace with why you are adopting *(e.g., infertility, lack of partner)?*
2. What will the impact of adoption be on your current or future biological children *(if appropriate)?*
3. What do you know and not know about the process of adoption?
4. What information do you need to obtain regarding adoption?
5. What questions do you have about adoption—before, during, and after adoption occurs?
6. What are the benefits of adoption?
7. What are your worries or concerns about adoption?
8. How can you minimize those worries or concerns?
9. What parameters *(e.g., age, gender, ethnicity, health, prenatal care, disabilities, drug or alcohol exposure)* are important for you to set in terms of adoption criteria?
10. What type of adoption *(e.g., open)* are you comfortable with?
11. What will your family's and friends' response and reaction be to adoption? How will you deal with that?
12. What resources and support will you have access to throughout the adoption process and in the future?
13. Which method of adoption are you most comfortable with and confident in?

ANNIVERSARIES

My favorite time to use questions is when my husband and I celebrate our anniversary. We usually take turns asking each other questions and have done it often enough that we can be rather spontaneous and let the questions come as they may. For those who are more analytical and need time to think before responding, I suggest you provide the questions in advance.

These questions, paired with a great meal and an adult beverage or two (though not necessary), are the best aphrodisiac I know! If you need additional questions, check out the "Romance and Sex" chapter later in this book.

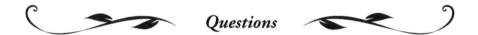

Questions

1. In the last year, what were the low point and high point for you? *(We always start with this one!)*
2. In the last year, what thoughtful, kind, or meaningful thing did I do for you unexpectedly that you really appreciated?
3. After _____ years, what still surprises you about me?
4. What is your favorite part of my body?
5. What is your wish for me this year? *(Be careful with this one. Make sure you don't use it as an opportunity to criticize or request that your partner change in some way.)*
6. What do you see as my greatest strength professionally, personally, and as a parent? *(Ask each question individually.)*
7. What was your greatest fear about getting married, and did it come true?

8. What was your greatest hope, wish, or desire about getting married, and did it come true?
9. Which positive attributes do you see in _____ *(insert each child's name)* that you think came from me?
10. What do you want to accomplish as a couple over the next year?
11. What are three qualities of mine that most attracted you to me when we first met?
12. What are three qualities of mine that are most important to you now?
13. What is one thing we have accomplished together that has totally exceeded your expectations?
14. What's one thing we've accomplished together that doesn't surprise you?
15. When did you first know you wanted to marry me? Who was the first person you told?
16. What advice or words of wisdom would you give to a young couple or our children that you have learned from our marriage?
17. What remains on your marital bucket list?
18. What does each of us bring to the marriage?
19. What attributes and qualities do we share that strengthen our relationship?
20. What attributes and qualities are unique in each of us that strengthen our relationship?
21. How do you want to improve as a partner?
22. What is something you want in our relationship, but have been afraid to ask for?
23. In what ways are you a better person because of our marriage?
24. How do I make you laugh?
25. What have you learned as a result of being in a relationship with me?
26. How do I inspire you?
27. At what point in the marriage did you know it was going to last? *(I don't recommend you answer this question until you have been married at least ten to fifteen years.)*

AROUND THE CAMPFIRE

There is something about "the dark" that encourages intimacy. I found that to be true when my children were small and I would lie down with them at bedtime. What wasn't said or was held back during the day magically came to the surface once the lights were turned off. I have also experienced this same glow of intimacy during extended car rides but only after the sun set. It is as if the darkness allows us to be anonymous and vulnerable while at the same time feeling deeply connected to those sharing the dark with us. I think many of us are most comfortable being truly seen when we can't be seen at all.

Ironically one of the best places to feel this phenomenon is around a campfire. I say ironic because the atmosphere created by a campfire is not a result of darkness alone but a blend or contrast of light and dark. We are seen but not seen. Sitting around a campfire, a source of heat and comfort in and of itself, allows us to experience each other indirectly and in the safety of shadows.

Many times my family and friends have tried to explain the mesmerizing effect of a campfire. The best we could come up with is that it is a combination of factors. Our attraction to it is probably primitive, imprinted on our DNA thousands of years ago. Our forbearers knew that a campfire was life sustaining and a place for their clan to gather peacefully. It allowed for time to rest and restore so that they could be better prepared for whatever life brought them the next day. I'm not sure its meaning and purpose has changed much since then.

Whatever its origins, a campfire can often embolden the most reticent of us to share a story, sing a song, tell a joke, or reveal something personal. I know firsthand the spell it can have on a person. I, who cannot carry a tune in a bucket, will sing with gusto around a roaring campfire!

Below are questions that can be answered round-robin style around the campfire. Start with the fun and rather safe questions, and then, as you feel the magic of the campfire spread and envelope the group, try the more self-revealing questions.

Most of the questions below were created around the campfire at our place in Oregon. In fact, I must give credit where credit is due. Thank you, Mary Jo, Dallis, and Rhys, for providing this chapter with most of its questions, its authenticity, and all of its character!

 *Questions*

1. Who is your favorite band and why?
2. What movie is your favorite and why?
3. What book had the most impact on you?
4. What is your favorite camping experience?
5. Where is your favorite camping spot?
6. What was your favorite bedtime story growing up?
7. What is your favorite tree and why?
8. Which tree/animal/flower are you most like and why?
9. What animal do you admire most and why?
10. If you had to be a nocturnal animal, which one would it be?
11. What is your favorite dessert? Favorite dessert around a campfire?
12. What is your favorite meal made around a campfire?
13. What is the scariest story you ever heard around the campfire?
14. What are your favorite campfire songs? Are you willing to sing them for us or teach them to us?
15. What music, movie, or book had the most impact on you during your youth? Your early adulthood? Currently?
16. What is the best joke you heard around the campfire?
17. As a child, what did you fear most?
18. As an adult, what do you fear most?
19. What superstitions do you still hold on to?
20. If you had to survive out in the woods by yourself for a month, how would you do it? What would your strategy be? What three things would you wish to have with you to help you survive?
21. How do you think fire changed humankind's lives and experience?
22. What do you think exists beyond the stars?
23. Do you think there is life somewhere else in the universe? Why or why not?

24. What "mystery of life question" would you like answered most?
25. Who in this circle knows you the most? Explain.
26. What secret are you willing to share around this campfire?
27. How do you think the world was created?
28. What is on your "bucket list"?

PEGGY JENNINGS-SEVERE

BIRTHDAYS

A number of years ago I suggested we eliminate the giving of birthday cards within our immediate—and, in some cases, extended—family. I wish I could say I've done so because of my desire to be environmentally responsible and not waste paper, but that wasn't my main motivation. The idea appealed to me for two reasons.

My first epiphany came to me while I was dumping a handful of cards I had just received for my birthday into a recycling bin. At least I was environmentally responsible in that way. But as I tossed them, I realized how wasteful and expensive the practice of giving cards was. The life expectancy of a greeting card has got to be a week maximum. The only exception might be if your offspring gave you the card and only because it was his or her first attempt to write his or her name, or the card contained an abundance of Xs and Os. You're likely to keep a card such as this in some forgotten box, for an undetermined period of time, out of obligation or sheer parental guilt. But I'd venture to say that most greeting cards are tossed within one week of receiving them.

With a present, at least, once it's opened, you're likely to use it, wear it, or return it and in so doing get some value from it. But cards are different. Once the occasion is over, there's no ongoing purpose for them. Furthermore, cards aren't typically made by the giver, nor is the sentiment generally written by him or her—which is the second reason I decided that cards were unnecessary in my family. Store-bought cards are unoriginal and therefore impersonal. When it's my birthday, I want the sentiment to count. I want it to come from the heart of the one giving it to me. So no more printed cards for us—just "verbal cards" that mean something to the giver and receiver!

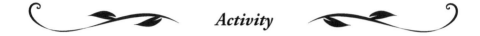

Activity

Birthday Verbal Cards

This activity is simple. When the birthday girl, boy, man, or woman is ready, everyone sits in a circle. I usually ask, "Who wants to begin?" I do this because some people take longer to form their thoughts and ideas, especially if they've never done this exercise before. Each person, when ready, completes the following statement.

"What I appreciate about _____ is…" (no sarcasm is allowed). Note: I encourage everyone present, regardless of age, to participate, even if he or she can say only one thing. I've found this to be an excellent way for young children, teens, and young adults to learn the language of friendship and love and to be able to share it in a safe environment.)

Next, ask the person celebrating his or her birthday to answer one or more of the following questions.

Looking Backward

1. What have you learned of significance in your _____ years that you want to share with us?
2. What are you most proud of related to your life thus far?
3. What abilities or attributes have you acquired thus far in your life?
4. If you were an impartial observer, how would you describe yourself at the age of five, your current age, and what you think you might be like in twenty years?
5. In what ways have you exceeded your expectations of where you would be by this point in your life?
6. In what ways did you think you would be farther along by this point in your life?
7. Knowing what you know now, what advice would you give your younger self?
8. In reviewing your life, of what are you most proud?

Looking Forward

1. In what way do you want to celebrate your birthday this year?
2. What are you looking forward to in the coming year?
3. What question about your life do you want answered in the coming year?

4. What do you want to give up this coming year?
5. What do you want to gain or achieve this coming year?
6. What is the best part and most challenging part of being at this stage of your life?
7. What is on your bucket list?
8. What is left to accomplish and when do you want to accomplish it?
9. What abilities or attributes do you have yet to acquire or master?
10. In anticipating your future, what excites you most?

BOOK CLUBS

Book clubs are one of the greatest social inventions that have occurred within my lifetime. Don't let the name deceive you though. Book clubs have very little to do with books. At least that is the case with the Stansbury Court Book Club.

The selection process to join the Stansbury Court Book Club is rather onerous and demanding, but once you are in, you're in. Unless you do something outrageous (like drink more than your share of the chardonnay or come empty handed for the holiday pot luck and gift exchange), you are guaranteed a lifetime membership. But first you have to be invited into "the club."

Though I never aspired to be in a sorority while I was in college and thus have no real knowledge of the inner workings of sororities, I suspect our selection process is a little like rush week in that our group chooses you, not the other way around. We have very little turnover, so our rush week happens, on average, every leap year.

When I think about it, though, our selection process is a little on the mysterious side. If someone wants to join our group, she tells a current member, who then brings forth her name to the group. We then ask pertinent questions, such as whether they have realistic expectations or are the type that expects everyone to buy the book, read it, and discuss it at length. If the answer is the latter, then she is immediately eliminated. We also want to know if she is open minded, has a sense of humor, is sensitive to others' feelings, and is able to flow with various opinions. If yes, then there is a good shot she will be inducted into the Stansbury Court Book Club!

Generally, I am someone who fights for inclusiveness, but my book club is one of the few times that I appreciate our rather cautious and careful selection process. Nevertheless, our group is rather eclectic. Our ages run a span of thirty years, and though we tend to lean on the liberal side, we do have one Republican among us. We also have several therapists—which means free counseling—a couple of artists, an eighty-year-old with a private pilot's license, many world travelers, and more than a few heterosexuals. And what we all have in common is a shared love and respect for each other that is priceless and worth protecting.

Because we have been together for nearly two decades, we have little trouble getting a meaningful conversation going. Talking about the book and staying on topic is another matter. So I asked these twelve wonderful women, who have been there for me during my darkest moments and my greatest triumphs, what questions we could ask ourselves each month that would help us to get the most from the book that most of read and that would keep us a little more focused. Here are their suggestions.

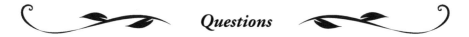 *Questions*

1. Would you like white wine or red wine?
2. Which character did you enjoy the most/least?
3. Which character did you identify with the most/least?
4. Was the protagonist someone you would like to know?
5. Do any of the characters in the book have traits of people you know?
6. What emotions did you feel while reading the book?
7. Was anything left unfinished, unsaid, undeveloped?
8. What did you think of the author's writing style?
9. Did the writing style work and flow for you?
10. What did you learn from the book? About the subject? About yourself?
11. What character, relationship, or subplot do think drove or was most important to the book?
12. How many pages did it take before you became fully engaged with the book? Why?
13. Did reading the book change your thinking about a particular topic or theme contained in the book?
14. In your opinion, was anything (plot, character) left unfinished, unsaid, or underdeveloped?
15. What do you think the author's intent or motive was for writing the book?

16. If you could meet the author, what question or questions would you ask her or him?
17. Would you read a sequel to the book? Why or why not?
18. Would you read another book written by this author? Why or why not?
19. Would you like some more wine?

CHRISTMAS

Like many people, I have always considered Christmas, and all of the hype leading up to it, to be one of the best times of the year. What's not to like? Plenty of great food and sugar-filled treats, catchy music you can sing along to, and twinkling lights of various colors that brighten even the dreariest of winter days. On top of that, if you have been mostly good and not too naughty, you are given carefully wrapped gifts—often more than one.

But some years, nay, most years, Christmas—the commercial version anyway—has a hard time living up to my expectations. I keep wanting and frankly expecting the Hallmark kind of Christmas, where the well-groomed, multigenerational, and exceedingly happy family is standing around a baby-grand piano singing, with perfect pitch, Christmas carols. I don't know about you, but my real-life Christmas seems to pale in comparison. I've never been able to sing, my parents are long gone, and many of my family members need their "happy pills" in order to achieve any yuletide spirit.

Nonetheless, we do our best to carve out time during the hustle and bustle of the season for activities and traditions that are both fun and joyful. And each year I make sure to embrace the spiritual side of the holidays as well. For instance, I love attending the candlelight service at my church, which is held late in the evening on Christmas Eve in the small, intimate chapel. The service grounds me, reminds me of the origins and greater meaning of Christmas, and allows my family and me something we rarely get: quiet and reflective time together. Without this infusion of the sacred, I feel like a bit of an imposter celebrating Christmas.

So in thinking about this chapter and considering ways to increase the opportunities to share quiet and reflective time with those I love and cherish, it occurred to me that I could achieve this by using an old tradition (the Advent calendar) in a new way. Instead of opening the date on the Advent calendar and getting a candy or picture, why not have a question waiting for all to answer? This would provide time daily, leading up to December 25, for family and friends to share their thoughts, feelings, and memories in a focused and fun way. Now that is a gift, and one that doesn't cost a cent!

For those who celebrate Hanukkah or Kwanzaa, you may want to incorporate this activity leading up to the main event (e.g., eight days of Hanukkah). Obviously, you will need to change or modify some of the questions to fit the occasion and religion.

 *Activity*

December 1	December 2	December 3	December 4	December 5
How are you going to make the holidays special and meaningful this year for yourself?	How are you going to make the holidays special and meaningful this year for others?	What do you want most from Santa?	What is your favorite Christmas book or story?	If you had no money or decorations, how would you celebrate the holidays?

December 6	December 7	December 8	December 9	December 10
What is your favorite Christmas movie? Why?	How does Christmas or the Advent season change you for the better?	What was the best gift you have ever received?	What is your favorite Christmas memory?	If you could change or add one new activity or tradition to make the holidays more meaningful, what would it be?

December 11

Who in the family or circle of friends has the most Christmas spirit? Explain.

December 12

If you had limitless money and resources, what special gift would you give the world?

December 13

What is your favorite Christmas tradition?

December 14

What was the oddest/silliest/most unique Christmas gift you have ever received?

December 15

Do you have the Christmas spirit yet? Why or why not?

December 16

What do Christmas and the Advent season mean to you religiously, spiritually, and/or culturally?

December 17

What is the best Christmas gift that someone could give you right now that doesn't cost a thing?

December 18

What is your favorite Christmas carol or song? Why?

December 19

Is your faith tested or strengthened, or both, during the Advent season?

December 20

What is the best gift you have ever given?

December 21

What is your favorite Christmas dish or food? Why?

December 22

What was the most unique or creative Christmas gift you have ever given?

December 23

What is one kind and unexpected thing you did for someone this season? What was his or her reaction?

December 24

What do you think Jesus's birth means to you and the world?

December 25

In what ways would you like to emulate or be more like Jesus?

CONVERSING WITH YOUR CHILDREN

I believe that one of my parents' greatest legacies or gifts to us, their children, was their genuine interest in us. Especially as we reached adolescence and early adulthood, my mother and father were both eager to know what we thought and why. A lively intellect was valued by both my parents, but I was also lucky to have a mother who was willing and able to traverse the somewhat messier realm of feelings. Either way, I was lucky to have such a ready and enthusiastic outlet for my youthful observations, my teenage angst, and my emerging and malleable world view.

As I mentioned before, my father's interest was not always evenly distributed among us kids, but once my brothers left home for college and I was their only child remaining, his focus began to shift to me, and I began to sense his keen interest in who I was and what made me tick mentally.

My parents demonstrated both their curiosity and respect for us by—what else—asking us sometimes general and other times pinpoint questions and seeking our opinions. Early on, I remember being honored when they would ask us where we wanted to go to dinner, if we had vacation ideas, and for whom we would vote for president if we could. They not only asked the questions, but listened to our answers and took them into consideration. And as we got older, they, especially my father, would challenge our viewpoints, but in a way that made us think more deeply and maturely, even if we resented it at times.

My advice, then, is to avoid the monologues and speeches and keep the lectures to a minimum. Instead, engage your children, nieces, nephews, or grandchildren in conversations that are fun, two way, and informative.

I have tried to organize the questions below, starting with those that are most appropriate for the younger set and ending with questions most appropriate for teenagers and young adults.

Questions

1. How was your day *(my mom's daily and favorite question when we came home from school)?*
2. What was the best part of your day?
3. What was your least favorite or most challenging part of the day?
4. Who do you enjoy playing with most at school? Why?
5. What is your favorite meal?
6. What is your favorite dessert?
7. What/where would you like to:
   - Go to dinner?
   - Take a vacation?
   - Watch on TV?
   - Read?
   - See at the movies?
   - Purchase as a pet?
8. What is the best part of your school day?
9. What subject in school do you enjoy most?
10. What subject in school is most difficult or challenging at this time?
11. What are you looking forward to most this:
    - School year?
    - Winter holiday?
    - Spring break?
    - Summer vacation?
12. Who are your heroes?
13. What/Who is your favorite:
    - Book?
    - Author?
    - Musician?
    - Actor?
    - Song?
    - Band?
    - Artist?
    - TV show?

14. If you were to rate how happy or content you are with your life right now on a scale of one to ten *(ten being you couldn't get any happier and one being "life sucks")*, what number would you give it? *(This question has been my go-to question with my introverted son, who doesn't easily or often express or share his emotions.)*
15. If you could do anything in this very moment, what would you be doing?
16. Who are your best friends (female and male)?
17. If you could change one thing about yourself, what would it be and why?
18. If you could change one thing about your parents, what would it be and why?
19. If you could change one thing about your family, what would it be and why?
20. If you could change one thing about the world, what would it be and why?
21. What is something you do really well?
22. What is something you want to learn or improve upon?
23. If you could be anyone, have anything, or do anything, who/what would it be?
24. What are your thoughts related to *(insert social and political issues of the day)?*
25. What are you most grateful for?
26. What are you most dissatisfied with?
27. What are you thinking/feeling?
28. How can we support you?
29. How can you help yourself?
30. What do you want most?
31. How can you earn/achieve/make it happen?

PEGGY JENNINGS-SEVERE

CONVERSING WITH YOUR PARENTS, GRANDPARENTS, AND ELDERS

In the fall of 1991, I borrowed a heavy and clunky video camera, placed it on a tripod, and proceeded to interview my father and then my mother. They were seventy-four and seventy, respectively, at the time. I provided them with a list of questions and topics in advance—ones I wanted them to cover—but I assured them that really anything was admissible.

I chose to approach the interview in a chronological order, starting at their birth and first memories and ending somewhere near 1991. Once we started, I sometimes let them wander with their thoughts, while other times I reined them back in. I often asked for clarification or inquired about specifics, especially names, dates, and locations. Sometimes I asked probing questions so they would cover aspects of their lives in more depth. I shared laughter with them when they recalled something funny and sadness when they spoke of loss. I learned a lot—more than I expected.

I lost both my parents a decade later and within two-and-a-half years of each other. I miss them every day. But I haven't lost them entirely, because I have their recorded autobiographies. Oddly enough I don't feel sad when I watch the tapes. Hearing their voices, seeing their mannerisms, and feeling their "essence" gives me great joy and comfort.

I have a couple of suggestions, though, about how to conduct interviews. Whomever you are interviewing, have the person do it with you alone. If someone else is present, often the interviewee will censor his or her answers or get distracted by comments from the observer.

It's important to prepare your interviewee well. As I mentioned, be sure to give the person the list of questions and topics in advance so he or she can spend time thinking about the answers and jot down notes, as my father did. This again ensures that the content will be thorough and well thought out. Inform the interviewee as to how much time he or she will have to answer the questions, and remind the person periodically of the time remaining so he or she can determine how much emphasis he or she wants to give a certain topic.

Finally, feel free to interrupt (when appropriate) to ensure there is no confusion or lack of understanding. After all, this may be the last time you'll ask the person these questions or hear his or her answers.

Questions

Early Years

1. What are the most cherished and significant memories and events of your life?
2. What was your first memory?
3. Where were you born? *(Ask for the city, region, country, and birth location, such as hospital, home, etc.)*
4. Who was present at your birth?
5. Where did you live as a baby, child, and teenager? Ask for addresses if possible.
6. What was your neighborhood like when you were growing up?
7. Did you have siblings? If so, what were their names, and what did you like most about them?
8. Who were your first friends?
9. What did you do for fun?
10. Who lived in your home?
11. Did you have pets? If so, what kind? What were their names?
12. What were your town, city, and community like? What was the approximate population? Were there special places where you liked to go?
13. What was happening economically during your childhood?
14. Which major political or social events do you remember while growing up?
15. What impact did the economy and major political or social events have on your family, neighborhood, and life?
16. Which jobs, chores, or responsibilities did you have as a kid?
17. Did you get paid for them? If so, how much?
18. Were you able to keep your own money and spend it as you liked?

School Years

1. Which schools did you attend? *(Ask for addresses here too.)*
2. How many students were in these schools?
3. Which extracurricular activities did you participate in?
4. Did you play sports? If so, which ones? What was your favorite and why?
5. Did you play an instrument or sing in the choir?
6. What were your forms of entertainment *(e.g., radio, TV, movies, books)?*
7. How did girls and boys hang out, meet each other, and date?
8. Who was your first girlfriend or boyfriend? How long did the relationship last? What ended it?
9. Did you ever go against your parents' wishes? Explain.
10. Did you ever get into trouble? If so, what happened?
11. Did you ever run away? If so, why and what happened?
12. What was your relationship like with your parents and grandparents? What were their personalities like?
13. Did you ever get teased as a child or have a nickname?
14. Did you enjoy school?
15. What kind of student were you?
16. What was your first means of transportation?
17. What was your first car?
18. Did you graduate from junior high? High school?

College Years (If Applicable)

1. What was the cost of college when you attended, and how did you pay for it?
2. Did you belong to clubs, fraternities, sororities, or service clubs?
3. While attending college, where did you live? What was the cost of rent?
4. What was your major? Did you ever change it?
5. What jobs did you have in college?
6. How long did it take you to graduate from college?
7. What did you like and dislike about college?

Armed Forces (If Applicable)

1. When and where did you serve?
2. Were you drafted or did you enlist?
3. What was your rank?
4. Did you ever experience combat? If so, what was it like?
5. What did you learn from your experience in the service?
6. If you had a choice, would you do it again? Why or why not?
7. What was one of the most significant events or experiences during your time in the service?

Adult Years

1. Were you or are you a sports fan? A music fan? What were or are your favorite teams, bands, and performers?
2. What was your first job as an adult? *(Ask the person to describe the job, the pay, and all other subsequent jobs.)*
3. Where did you meet your spouse or partner?
4. How did you know he or she was "the one"?
5. What were your engagement and wedding like?
6. What have been the greatest joys and challenges associated with being married?
7. What and where was the first home you bought?
8. Did you have children? Why or why not?
9. What were your experiences during the pregnancy and birth?
10. Have you traveled? If so, where? Have you had any especially unique or memorable traveling experiences?
11. Have you been or are you a member of any political parties or groups? Have you ever run for political office?
12. What famous people have you met in your lifetime?
13. What are all of the cities in which you have lived?

Ethnic/Cultural Questions

1. What is your ethnic/cultural background?
2. Which of your ancestors immigrated? When did they immigrate and from where?
3. What have been some of the adjustments, challenges, or prejudices that you and/or your ancestors faced?
4. What social or political issues or policies affected you and/or your ancestors or relatives?
5. Were any of your ancestors or relatives gay?
6. Were you or any of your ancestors or relatives adopted?
7. Did you or any of your ancestors or relatives have a disability?
8. What is your family's religious heritage?
9. What are your spiritual beliefs?
10. Have you or your ancestors ever been discriminated against as a result of ethnicity, culture, nationality, sexual orientation, disability, or religion?
11. Were you or any of your ancestors or relatives detained involuntarily due to ethnicity, culture, nationality, sexual orientation, disability, or religion *(e.g., relocation camps, concentration camps, reeducation camps, forced therapy, or institutionalization)*?

General Questions

1. What have been the best of times and worst of times for you?
2. Have you or any of your ancestors or relatives been in jail or imprisoned?
3. Have you ever been a hero? If so, explain.
4. How have you made a positive difference in your family, community, and the world?
5. What have been the biggest changes you have experienced *(social, economic, political, and scientific)* since your birth?
6. What has been your greatest achievement?
7. What has been your greatest disappointment?
8. What is your concept of death? Do you believe in life after death? Do you believe in reincarnation?
9. What advice would you give to future generations?

CULTURAL CONVERSATIONS

Years ago, I created a course titled "College and Life Success" that was designed for first-year college students. I also had the privilege of teaching the course for over ten years. The curriculum included topics you would predict in a course created to assist young adults and returning students be successful, such as time and money management, learning styles, and goal setting.

In creating the course, I also understood that if my mission was to help young and not-so-young adults become successful in college and in life, I needed to prepare them for the world at large. This may sound like a rather nebulous and at the same time grandiose goal, but as an educator I was familiar with the statistics and knew that the world my students were acquainted with in rural Northern California was not the world in which they were likely to live and work.

For instance, I knew from research that college students can be expected to change first their majors and then their jobs numerous times during their academic and professional lifetimes. I was also aware that the job they were likely to hold ten years after graduation did not exist while they were attending college. Most importantly, I was absolutely certain that most of my students were, upon graduation, more likely to move to an urban location to find a job than they were to remain in their local hometown.

But no matter where they lived or what their occupations ultimately were, I knew that employers wanted graduates who knew how to work in teams and how to live, socialize, and work with people of different ages, ethnicities, religions, nationalities, sexual orientations, and more. Bottom line, if I wanted my students to be successful, I knew I had better prepare them for change and diversity.

How I approached getting my students familiar with the unfamiliar was by having them complete a rather involved and time-consuming assignment titled "The Adopt-an-Identity Project." I don't know where I got the title, but I began the assignment by sharing with them a model of multiculturalism that I snagged at a conference years earlier.

The model is simple but I think right on. The premise is that there are four stages that we must traverse in order to be fully multicultural and versed in another culture other than our own. Those stages in a nutshell are:

1. Isolation—No interest or knowledge of cultures, ethnicities, or religions other than one's own. Belief in the superiority of one's own culture, ethnicity, religion, etc.

2. Inquiry—Blossoming interest in other cultures, ethnicities, or religions but done from a safe distance (e.g., through reading books, viewing movies, attending events, eating at restaurants, etc.).

3. Contact—Interacting in a significant way with people from other cultures, ethnicities, or religions. Must involve face-to-face contact and result in conversations that allow for deep and meaningful understanding of the underlying values, traditions, beliefs, and history that form the foundation of that culture, ethnicity, or religion.

4. Multiculturalism—Having acquired the skills, knowledge, and language (if applicable) to interact with another culture, ethnicity, religion, etc., as an "insider" or member would.

I would really get on my soapbox when I described the contact stage because it is at the contact stage where true understanding can begin and, as a result, prejudice and stereotypes can be slowly eroded and ultimately eliminated.

Then we would discuss protocol and how and what questions to ask. This can be a sensitive issue. Some people are thrilled and quite honored that you want to know more about them and the group of which they are a member. But others, especially when they are a member of a group that has been maligned, misunderstood, or suffered widespread and institutional oppression, violence, and injustice can be very cautious or unwilling. So I am going to tell you what I told my students. Before initiating a conversation focused on culture, make sure that you:

- Are aware of your motives. What I mean by this is, be sure that you are coming from a place of respect and genuine interest and not out of morbid curiosity or a desire to reaffirm your preexisting stereotypes.
- Ask permission. For many people from underrepresented or misunderstood groups, it takes courage and a lot of energy to teach the rest of us about their group. It also feels like a tremendous responsibility

or even a burden to represent an entire population (in actuality, it's impossible to do). And, some people just want to fit in, and to be asked to talk about what makes them different isn't something they enjoy doing. If they say no, don't take it personally. Try again at another time or approach someone else.

- Let them know the reason for your interest. Think this through before you speak. Saying you have always wanted to meet someone gay may be off-putting. Instead, you may want to say, "I have been reading more and more about gay rights, and I would like to ask you some questions about your experience as a gay man. Is this a good time, and are you OK with that?"
- Start with safe questions (ones that you would feel comfortable asking and answering) and assess their receptiveness before broaching the potentially more difficult and emotionally laden questions that require a level of comfort and trust to have been established.
- Thank them for their willingness and candor.

Regardless of what you say or how you approach it, the most important thing is that you do so with authenticity and sensitivity. If and when someone shares with you their experience, no matter what it is, accept it as a gift. They have entrusted to you their life story—to an extent—which always needs to be appreciated and affirmed. Last, be ready to answer questions about your ethnicity, culture, or religion. After all, turnaround is fair play.

So if you have a neighbor, coworker, new family member, or potential friend and you want to really learn who they are and all that may imply, begin by asking one or more of these questions and, in so doing, initiating the contact stage.

Please note that not all questions will apply to every group or situation, so choose accordingly and know that I use the term group in the most general sense. Group can refer to a religion, ethnicity, culture, socioeconomic status, sexual orientation, or other affiliation.

Last, I want to thank the many students who have graced my classrooms and who together helped develop many of the following questions.

Questions

General Questions

1. How do you define being (insert ethnicity, religion, sexual orientation, etc.)?
2. What are the most important things I need to know about your group?
3. What are some common misperceptions *(good or bad)* about your group?
4. In what ways are you connected/disconnected from others from your group?
5. What is one thing you want me to know about your group?

History

1. What is the history *(major events, periods of great significance, leaders who had important impact)* of your group? *(Don't be surprised if someone is not familiar with his or her group's own history, especially if he or she comes from an underrepresented group whose history is not addressed in traditional schools.)*
2. When did you or your family move to the area/country *(if immigration was involved)* and what was your/their experience like? What was the motivation behind the move?
3. What were the biggest obstacles and advantages in moving here?
4. What adjustments or accommodations, if any, have you or your group made as a result of relocation?
5. When were you first aware of the uniqueness of your *(insert group affiliation)*? What was the occasion, and what impact did it have on you?
6. Who, if anyone, has been your mentor and teacher related to being *(insert group affiliation)*?
7. As a member of your group, where do you feel most comfortable, safe, and accepted?
8. Where do you feel the least comfortable, safe, or accepted?

Accomplishments

1. What are you most proud of related to your group?
2. What significant accomplishments has your group achieved?
3. In what ways are you, the community, the country, the world, better off because of your group and its accomplishments?
4. How has being a member of your group helped you in achieving your goals and dreams?
5. How has being a member of your group blocked or delayed your ability to achieve your goals and dreams?

Education

1. What kind of training or education have you received regarding your group?
2. How does your group perceive or value education? Higher education? Are there different expectations based on gender?
3. How is the educational system you grew up in similar or dissimilar to the one you are experiencing now?
4. Have you ever had obstacles as a result of your group affiliation that have interfered with your education?
5. What is/was school like for you?
6. What sacrifices or adaptations have you had to make to further your education?
7. Does your family/group support extracurricular activities? How or how not?
8. Has anyone else in your family attended college? How does this influence your own college experience?
9. How does your upbringing differ from your parents'? Does this create any problems or conflicts?
10. How does your family feel about you attending college?
11. Does your family have an impact on your education? Do they support your choice to attend college? How?
12. In what ways, if at all, do your culture, family, and friends serve as obstacles to your academic success?

Peer and Group Affiliation

1. Do you tend to socialize more with your peers from your group? Why or why not?
2. What are the stated and unstated expectations you feel from your peer group?
3. Do you ever feel like deviating from those expectations? When and how? What happens when you do?
4. Do your peers have expectations of you in terms of dress, speech, behaviors, and/or obligations? What are their expectations, and how do you feel about and respond to them?
5. In what ways are you supported and encouraged by your peers?
6. In what ways are you stifled or held back by your peers?
7. Do you have a formal or informal network of your peers from your group? How does that network work?
8. Has it been easy or difficult to initiate and maintain relationships with people outside of your group?
9. What social challenges, if any, do you face making friends or dating outside your group?

10. What, if anything, have you found to be helpful in making friends or dating outside your group?
11. Do you ever experience social isolation as a result of being a member of your group?
12. Where and with whom do you feel most safe, secure, accepted, and authentic? *(You can answer each separately.)*
13. How often, if ever, are you the only one in a group setting who represents your specific group? What is that like for you?
14. When you are together with peers from your group, how do others (not from your group) react or respond?
15. Does your community provide opportunities and locations for peers from your group *(and others, if appropriate)* to congregate and socialize? What impact does that have on you and your peers?

Culture

1. What are you most proud of as it relates to your group?
2. How hard or easy was it for you to come to the United States and adapt to this culture?
3. What were the biggest obstacles in immigrating or getting to your current location?
4. How did you feel when you first moved here? Did you experience any cultural shock? Explain.
5. How have your cultural beliefs and values helped or hindered your schooling?
6. Have you been able to meet all your dietary, health, cultural, and/or religious needs in this community? Explain.
7. Have you felt any advantages or benefits as a result of your race, gender, age, disability, religion, etc.?
8. What aspects about your own group do you most like/dislike?
9. What differences have you noticed between your group and others?
10. What would you like to tell people about your group?

Traditions

1. What are some special celebrations, holidays, and activities that your culture celebrates?

Prejudice and Discrimination

1. What are your experiences with prejudice?
2. What are your experiences with discrimination?
3. Do you feel that you have been unfairly judged as a result of your ethnicity, age, religion, disability, and/or gender *(insert additional groups as needed)*? If yes, what were the circumstances?
4. Have you had to deal with discrimination in school, at work, or in the community? Please explain.
5. Can you share with me an experience when you have felt singled out due to your race, gender, age, disability, religion, etc.?
6. Have you ever been physically and/or verbally threatened by members of another ethnic/religious/social group? Please explain.
7. Have you ever felt profiled? If yes, please explain.
8. Have you had experience with systematic discrimination or oppression *(e.g., justice, banking/lending, housing, medical, educational systems)?*
9. Have you ever actively boycotted, demonstrated, or worked to change these systems? If yes, please explain.
10. Have you ever participated in discrimination or oppression against another group?
11. What is your greatest hope for your group?
12. What is your greatest fear for your group?

DIVORCE/ENDING A RELATIONSHIP

Divorce is a game changer. It rocks our world and impacts almost every facet of our lives. And it is prevalent. The statistics aren't pretty. Last I looked, 40 percent to 50 percent of married couples in America end up divorced.

As we all know, the reasons for divorce are numerous and varied. Each of us brings our expectations and our baggage, resolved and unresolved, to the marriage. So it is not surprising that after the honeymoon period ends and the hard work begins, some reconsider their choice.

Another contributing factor is that we simply live longer (twenty-eight years longer) than we did a century ago. It is hard enough to react and adjust to the opportunities and challenges that arise at each stage of our own lives. But when you add a spouse or partner and children to the mix, life just gets exponentially more complicated and stressful. If you are married long enough, you are bound to ask yourself at some point, even if it is for just a moment, "Am I better off single?"

I have never witnessed—up close anyway—a couple enter into divorce cavalierly. There always seems to be a lot of soul searching first, and that is a good thing. So if you are beginning to question the longevity of your marriage/relationship, I first recommend a good counselor or therapist. It certainly can't hurt, and if you do ultimately end up choosing to divorce, you are more likely to navigate those choppy waters with more awareness, mutual respect, and solid ground rules.

In the meantime or in addition to counseling, begin by asking yourself and possibly your spouse or partner the questions from chapter 2, titled "Am I/Are We Ready to Commit?" You may quickly realize that the doubt you are experiencing is situational and temporary. Below are additional questions that might assist you during this time of personal and marital introspection and transition.

Questions

Considering Divorce

1. Am I a better person with or without my partner?
2. How will divorce realistically serve or better my quality of life now and in the future?
3. How will divorce realistically serve or better my partner's quality of life now and in the future?
4. How will divorce realistically serve or better my children's quality of life now and in the future?
5. What am I willing to do and not to do to save this marriage?
6. What am I expecting my partner to do and not to do to save this marriage?
7. What is my role or contribution to what is healthy and unhealthy in this relationship?
8. What have I learned about myself in relationships and what do I still need to learn?
9. What baggage or unfinished business did I bring to this marriage from my family of origin?
10. How will divorce impact me?
11. How will divorce impact my children *(if applicable)*?
12. How will divorce impact me financially?
13. How will divorce impact my lifestyle?
14. How will divorce impact our relationships with extended family and friends?
15. How will divorce impact our social life and shared friendships?
16. If I could rebuild our relationship, how would I go about doing it?
17. If I could regain something in our relationship that was lost, what would it be?

Choosing Divorce

1. How will my life be the same and different once divorced? *(I first heard this question asked of children of divorce, as often they will catastrophize divorce initially, believing that their entire life will change when in fact only certain aspects of it will.)*
2. What is my optimum divorce plan (much like a birth plan)?
3. What is my partner's optimum divorce plan? Are they compatible?
4. Who needs to know first that we are divorcing? Who is going to tell them?
5. What is the first thing we want and need to do to begin the process of divorcing?

6. Do we need an unbiased mentor/facilitator *(clergy member, therapist, court-appointed arbitrator)* to assist us through the process of divorcing?
7. What kind of emotional support will each of us need while going through the transition?
8. What will I need to do to become financially independent and secure?
9. How and when do we want to communicate during the divorce?
10. What, if any, ongoing contact do we want to maintain after the divorce?
11. How do we plan to coordinate future decisions and events for our children?
12. How do we want to divide our belongings and assets? Do we need outside and unbiased help to do so?
13. What do we want to do with the pets?
14. What kind of support does each of us need to help in the grieving process?
15. Is there a couple who has divorced in a seemingly successful and mutually respectful way that we could talk to for advice?
16. What do I need to learn and change about myself so as to not repeat and relive this experience and outcome in the future? *(I include this question because I have met too many people who blame their partner for the demise of their relationship and never do their own work, and as such are destined to repeat the same pattern.)*

EASTER/SPRING

I love spring and by association Easter. My Christian friends would probably question my priorities, but they are what they are. I love spring for many reasons. One reason may be because I was born in April and am an Aries, which happens to be the first sign in the zodiac calendar. I am also an enthusiastic San Francisco Giants fan and avid gardener. So after a long, gloomy winter of primarily indoor sports and nothing but pansies to enjoy, I look forward to spring training and spring planting. Last, I love the promise of longer days and shorter nights.

At a deeper level, I have always appreciated Easter as a religious holiday in that it represents to me the promise of life eternal, the transformation of darkness into light, and the chance to personally and spiritually start anew.

So in my mind, there is much to celebrate during this season and, as such, another wonderful opportunity to connect with self and those we love. The questions below will help you do just that. Print or write the questions out on slips of paper and place them in plastic Easter eggs along with the usual loot of marshmallow-stuffed bunnies, fuzzy chicks, loose change, and lottery tickets. Place the stuffed Easter eggs in a basket on the dining room table or hide them as part of the traditional Easter egg hunt. In our family, we hide eggs for the children and the adults!

Questions

1. What does each of the four seasons represent to you?
2. What season do you like best and why?
3. What does Easter and/or spring mean to you?
4. What animal best represents Easter/spring to you? Why?
5. What plant or flower best represents Easter/spring to you? Why?
6. What do you want born anew in yourself?
7. What do you want born anew in the world?
8. What Easter tradition do you enjoy most? Why?
9. What Easter food do you enjoy most? Why?
10. If you could create a new Easter tradition, what would it be?
11. What is something new that you would like to have happen in your life?
12. While experiencing winter, what were you waiting for most with the coming of spring?
13. Did you give up anything for Lent? If so, why did you chose that particular sacrifice?
14. Do you believe there needs to be a death, symbolic or real, before there is birth or renewal?
15. What do Jesus's death and resurrection mean to you? To the world?

EMPTY NESTERS

Like many parents of adult-age children these days, my husband and I have become empty nesters, not just once but several times. Both our daughter and son, along with their significant others, have left our home, returned, and left again. Though I don't want to jinx our current living situation nor give my children (who will read this book one day) the impression that I would not welcome them back should the need arise, I am feeling fairly confident that we have become permanent members of the empty-nester club.

Now is a good time to state publically that we also reserve the right, at a future date (particularly if we are broke and feeble), to occupy their extra bedroom and do so indefinitely.

If your last or only child is on the cusp of leaving home or has done so already, just know that each transition in life has its good points and bad points, and this situation is no exception. At first and in theory it sounds great—more privacy, more money, more time for self—but in reality there is a flip side to all that—more privacy (do I remember how to spend time with my significant other?), more money (an illusion), and more time (to do what?). The challenge of being a member of this club, as I see it, is to figure out how to fill the void left by children in a healthy and sustaining way.

The questions that follow are ones that my husband and I have asked ourselves and each other, sometimes more than once.

Questions

1. What do I miss the most about having children living at home?
2. What do I enjoy the most about not having children living at home?
3. What feels different without children at home?
4. What feels the same without children at home?
5. In what ways can we redirect "children time" to "couple time"?
6. How do I want to fill the void?
7. How do I not want to fill the void?
8. What new hobbies, interests, or volunteer work do I want to pursue?
9. What new or existing relationships do I want to create or nurture?
10. In what ways has our relationship with our child changed now that he or she no longer lives with us?
11. In what ways has our relationship with our child stayed the same?
12. How do I/we intend to stay connected in a healthy way with my/our child?
13. What new opportunities and traditions do we want to explore with our child?
14. How will I feel if my child wants to move back home?
15. What conditions would I need to set for that to happen?
16. How will I communicate these conditions or guidelines?

HEALTH ISSUES, HOSPITAL STAYS, AND DEATH

My father was a hypochondriac, convinced that every cold was going to turn into pneumonia, every hangnail was sure to result in gangrene, and abdominal cramping and general bloating meant stomach cancer. My mother, on the other hand, was stoic and rarely went to the doctor. Instead, she doctored herself using disturbing amounts of aspirin, Vicks VapoRub, and chugging—directly from the bottle—a white, chalky substance that I think and hope was antacid. I find myself somewhere in the middle—sure I am going to die one moment, while the next time just as confident that an aspirin, a Tums, or both will cure anything.

Typical of someone in my generation, I remember going to a doctor only once or twice before the age of twelve. Same with the dentist. If it didn't look broken or life threatening, at least to my mom, it didn't warrant medical attention. Even my childhood vaccinations were handled not in a doctor's office, but in the cafeteria of Magnolia Elementary School.

Later, in my late twenties, I was blessed with a good job that provided excellent medical insurance, and thus I was a little more open to using a variety of medical practitioners. By the time I was a working mother with two kids who attended the "Ear Infection and Chicken-Pox-Sharing Day Care" across town, going to the pediatrician or the walk-in health clinic became an almost weekly occurrence.

But none of this prepared me for the diagnosis that I received shortly after turning fifty. According to many developmental psychologists, the decade of the fifties (the new forties) is when you are likely to, for the first time, greet and ultimately (if you do your personal and spiritual work) shake hands with your mortality.

My introduction was none too gentle. The candles had barely been blown out on my birthday cake when mortality came knocking on my door. I was celebrating the beginning of my sixth decade in the Northern California wine country with a dozen women friends from all over the West Coast. I was pulling on my pajamas after our first night together and felt a tug, similar to a snag in a sweater, just above my left nipple. I instantly began to search with my fingers and found what is so aptly described as a lump.

I was in disbelief. I kept feeling it over and over again to make sure I hadn't imagined it. After a while it began to hurt from all of my probing. The next morning after breakfast, while we all waited for our spa treatments, I had many of my friends feel it and ask what they thought. No one knew for sure, but all agreed I needed to have it checked out as soon as possible, and that is just what I did. A week later, I was diagnosed with breast cancer. Six weeks later, after a full-body scan, I learned that I had thyroid cancer as well. Hello, mortality!

What is ironic is that I have been fascinated by death my entire adult life. My interest in death is, in part, because I find death to be the ultimate mystery of life. We know that we will all die, we just don't know when, where, or how, and no one can tell us with certainty what awaits us when we do. Yet for such an intriguing topic that represents a universal, unavoidable, lives-changing experience, why does it still remain, for many of us, a taboo subject?

So over the years, I have searched for opportunities to think about and discuss death. I have read several books about people who had been clinically declared dead, but later regained consciousness or were resuscitated and remembered their experience of "death." These books have given me great comfort, as nearly each person who shared their experience of "death" returned feeling renewed, optimistic, and confident that there is indeed an afterlife and that it is a blissful one.

Fortunately for me, the subject of death was also relevant and necessary to my first profession, counseling. After grad school, I got a job in an adolescent and family counseling center, and while employed there I requested funding and time off to participate in a weeklong training titled "Living with Dying." A year later, I attended a conference that included a keynote speech by Elisabeth Kubler-Ross, the well-known and respected author and expert on death and dying. Her work, especially in identifying the stages of grief, was incredibly helpful in my work and life.

I was also fortunate years later to travel to India with a small group led by a Tibetan Buddhist teacher, Losang, who was once a monk and had served as the personal assistant to the Dalai Lama. My Western and predominately Christian view of death and the afterlife was given a healthy infusion of Eastern-Buddhist ideology. After my return from India and during one of Losang's many visits to my community, he sat down with my daughter and me and let us ask him questions specifically about death.

Though always curious in a hypothetical and academic way about death and the traditions and practices surrounding it, I had no practical experience with it until much later in my life. For instance, I had never been to a funeral until I was twenty and did not go to one again for many years thereafter. Nor had I lost anyone close to me, in that life-changing way, until I was in my forties. Thus, I was ill prepared when I lost my father, aunt, uncle, mother, best friend, and secretary within a four-year span, nor for my bout with cancer two years later. Instead of death being an interesting and hypothetical topic, it had become a serious and real thing. As you might suspect, one of the ways I coped with my fear and incredible grief during this six-year period was to ask a lot of questions. I also learned, through trial and error, when not to ask questions but to simply accept death for what it was. Not so easy.

So when I told my hairdresser that I had started to write Life Talks—The Conversations Continue, she immediately asked me to include a chapter with questions that allow and facilitate what are often difficult and awkward conversations with friends and family members (or yourself) who may be going through difficult and in some cases life-threatening illnesses. At first, the idea intimidated me, but it also, as you might have guessed by now, intrigued me. So here goes. I have broken the chapter into three parts: personal health issues, supporting others with health issues, and death. I hope they prove helpful to you and in some small measure lighten your load.

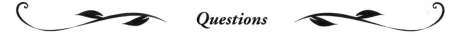

Questions

PERSONAL HEALTH ISSUES—Questions to Ask Your Health Provider

(When dealing with a serious or life-threating illness or diagnosis, whenever possible, make a list of questions prior to your medical appointments. I even asked my husband and children if they had questions they wanted me to ask my oncologists on their behalf. Secondly, always take someone with you to the appointment. He or she can take notes or be that additional pair of ears, so that when you mentally check out due to fear or information overload, you can ask him or her later what he or she remembers.)

1. What do I need to know about my condition/illness?
2. What are my options?

3. What are the side effects?
4. If you were me, what would you do?
5. If I wanted a second opinion, how would I go about getting one?
6. What are the nontraditional, non-Western treatment options?
7. What are the nontraditional, non-Western practices or services that will complement or ease the side effects of my traditional treatment approach?
8. What is the prognosis?
9. Where can I get support?
10. Where can I learn more (*books, online sites, chat rooms*)?
11. What online sites or books should I avoid (*outdated or not research-supported information, noncredible sources*)?
12. What can I expect?
13. If I have questions or concerns in between appointments/treatments, who can I contact?
14. Would you recommend counseling? Who would you recommend?
15. What support and/or counseling is there for my spouse and children?
16. What is the best I can expect?
17. What is the worst I can expect? (*Ask this question only if you really want to know.*)
18. Is there someone who has experienced my condition who would be willing to talk with me?
19. What's a question I haven't asked, but should have (*directed at health-care provider*)?
20. What is my greatest fear (*question to ask yourself and possibly share with health-care provider*)?

SUPPORTING OTHERS (Friends & Family Members) WITH HEALTH ISSUES

1. How are you?
2. Is this a good time to ask you about your illness/condition?
3. What can you tell me about your illness/condition?
4. When is your next appointment, and would you like me to accompany you?
5. What is your next appointment about? (*A friend suggested this question, which she uses with her father, who is hesitant to share too many details about his leukemia in an attempt to protect her. It's just probing enough to get more information without making her father too uncomfortable.*)
6. Would you like me to keep this confidential?
7. Are there others you would like me to tell or keep informed? (*When I was diagnosed with breast cancer and a month later with thyroid cancer, it was*

exhausting keeping everyone informed. I very much appreciated my husband keeping the family aware while a couple of designated people kept my friends and coworkers updated.)

8. What is the prognosis?
9. What are your feelings regarding your condition?
10. What are your feelings regarding your prognosis?
11. What are your feelings regarding your treatment?
12. What do you need?
13. Would it be helpful if I pick up groceries, take your children to school in the morning, establish a rotating dinner/meal service, mow your lawn? *(Offer suggestions, as the person may not even know what might help.)*
14. How can I support you now?
15. How can I support you in an ongoing way?
16. Who else needs my/our support while you go through this?
17. What would be the best way to check in with you?
18. What is your greatest fear?
19. What is your death plan *(i.e., what do you want in terms of a service or funeral and cremation or burial, etc.)?*
20. Are your finances in order?
21. Do you have any unfinished personal business? *(I asked my father this question shortly after we had a rather frank discussion about the seriousness of his condition. He ended up dictating a story to me, one that I had never heard before. I later typed it up and sent to the person for whom it was intended, my half-brother.*

DEATH

After my father's funeral and the lunch reception that followed, I was fortunate enough to go home and be surrounded by those I loved and trusted most: my mother, my brothers and their families, my best girlfriends, and our oldest couple friends, a pair with whom my husband and I had shared a duplex during our early marriage years. As often happens after an emotional day, people began to divide into groups, doing what they needed to do to shore themselves up. My mother went to bed, the teens congregated in the den, and we "middle-somethings" found ourselves in the living room, seated in a circle. Nothing lends itself more to round-robin questions than death, a small circle of your closest and most trusted friends and family, and raw emotions.

Keep in mind that you don't have to wait for a death to occur before you share the reflections that these questions generate. It would be ideal to have had many of these conversations with the deceased person prior to his or her death. Sometimes, however, that isn't possible, and even if it were, it's nice to hear how others view this important person in your life.

Questions

1. What will you miss most about _____?
2. What did you learn from_____?
3. Do you remember a time when _____ disciplined or corrected you? What was the occasion, and what did you learn?
4. Do you remember a time when you laughed from the gut with _____?
5. What was the occasion, and what did you learn from it?
6. Do you remember a time when you cried with _____? What was the occasion, and what did you learn from it?
7. Do you remember a time when _____ helped you through a difficult time?
8. What were _____'s greatest qualities or strengths?
9. What odd or unique saying, phrase, or word do you associate with _____?
10. What was the best advice _____ ever gave you?
11. What do you think this person would say was his or her greatest accomplishment?
12. What legacy did _____ leave?
13. What's your favorite memory of _____?
14. What made _____ unique?
15. If you could say or ask _____ one thing, what would it be?
16. What was _____'s philosophy of life?
17. What did _____ value most?
18. Did you have any unfinished business with _____? (*This is a tricky question, one that can be both painful and cathartic, and must be asked only in a very safe environment.*)

HIGH SCHOOL REUNIONS

I wonder if there is anyone who in anticipation of his or her high school (or college) reunion does not have some anxiety. Regardless of whether it is your fifth, twentieth, or, in my case recently, fortieth reunion, I think we all spend a moment or two contemplating our stature in this world and whether it will measure up to the other attendees. The good thing about my impending fortieth reunion is that it has been so long since we graduated, we are now older and bound to be a little wiser about what is really important in life. Thus our need to impress will have hopefully chilled out a bit. As groovy as we may think we were or are, I suspect our discussions will no longer be about our job titles and income brackets but instead be more focused on the economy, our 401(k)s, our grandchildren, and the next road trip—with or without an RV.

So the good news is that I no longer worry about being groovy or righteous. The bad news, though, is that I still harbor a desire to be a little foxy. Not in an eighteen-year-old miniskirt way, but in a boy-she-has-held-up-well-for-her-age kind of way. I am a tad worried that I may not be able to pull it off. For instance, at a recent professional conference I attended, I met a woman who knows my brother. She had the audacity to ask me if I was the older sister. Wrong! My brother Ross is older by six years, and I told her so!

Her comment hit a nerve though. Upon my return from the conference, I asked my hairdresser whether my decision two years ago to let my hair color go to its natural state—whatever that might be now—was a smart one. I also found myself—for the first time—noticing advertisements for under-eye creamers and concealers. I rarely wear makeup, but with my high school reunion quickly approaching, I gave it some thought. As for the extra forty pounds, I didn't even consider it. It was too late.

We all have insecurities, and putting mine aside for a moment, I realize that my hope and intention is to spend less time concealing and more time revealing. I want, as you might suspect by now, to make real connections with those who are willing, and the only way I am going to accomplish this is by using—you guessed it—questions. Well-thought-out and appropriately probing questions.

I think the questions below can also help during events where time is limited, but your desire to reconnect is not! As always, start with the safer questions, then move to the more revealing ones once trust and openness have been established. Be ready to share as well.

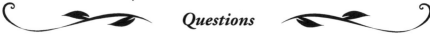 *Questions*

Questions about High School/College

1. What do you remember most about high school?
2. What year in high school was the best and the worst for you?
3. What was the most satisfying thing you did in high school?
4. What did you accomplish or try that surprised you?
5. What was the funniest moment for you in high school?
6. If you could change one thing about your high school experience what would it have been?
7. What was one goal you had in high school that you met and what was one that was left unfulfilled?
8. Who knew you best in high school? Have you kept in touch?
9. Looking back, in what way were you understood and misunderstood in high school?
10. What was one of the most embarrassing times in high school? (*Sometimes the embarrassment and shame we carry with us for years lessens or evaporates when we give it a voice, laugh about it, and set it free.*)
11. If you had high school to do over, what would you do differently and the same?

Questions about Life after High School

1. What are your goals for this next chapter in your life?
2. What is on your bucket list?
3. What has been your greatest accomplishment(s) (*aside from kids and job*)?
4. What has happened in your life since high school that surprises you the most?
5. What would I be surprised to learn about you?

6. What high school dreams came true? Which did not?
7. What ever happened to...?
8. What did you do immediately after high school, and how long did it take you to find your path/purpose?
9. What is the most daring and safest thing you have done since high school?
10. What advice would you give, or have you given, to entering freshman about high school?

As it turned out, I was unable to attend the reunion due to another commitment, but I am now armed and ready for my fiftieth!

LONG-DISTANCE RELATIONSHIPS

Midway through writing this, my second book, I came down with a bad case of self-doubt. I questioned (of course) everything. Did I really want to invest more money into a project that was barely profitable now? If my first book hadn't landed on the New York Times best-sellers list yet, what made me think that a sequel would be any more successful? Did I really have something important to share or was I fooling myself? You get the drift. A full-blown pity party!

But as the universe often does, a timely intervention occurred. As I was walking across campus this spring, I ran into a colleague of mine that I had not seen for some time. We chitchatted for a while, and then all of a sudden her demeanor changed completely. She lit up and with great animation and hands flying said, "Oh, Peggy, I have been meaning to tell you that I lent your book to a student of mine." She went on to tell me that the student had recently met and fallen in love with a young man from Mexico. Unfortunately, this young man had to return home shortly after they met, but her student was determined to keep the new relationship alive. "She loves the book and is using it to keep the long-distance conversations going. I can't get it back from her." Needless to say, I thanked the instructor and told her that she had made my day.

Fortunately for this young couple, they have many ways to stay connected that were not available to my husband, Rhys, and me. Rhys was in the Marine Corps for four years and was stationed on the East Coast and in Japan while I was attending college on the West Coast. We had to rely on letters and the occasional and very expensive long-distance phone call.

I also can't help but think of my grandparents who met in 1909 when my grandmother came from Minneapolis to Seattle to visit family and attend the Alaska-Yukon-Pacific Expedition. My grandfather lived in Seattle and they met through mutual friends. After a rather short, but presumably passionate courtship, my grandmother returned home to Minnesota. They did not see each other again until five long years later, when my grandfather took the train to Minneapolis and married her—the love of his life! Those letters and telegraphs must have been pretty dang good.

And now decades and almost a century later, my own son finds himself on the East Coast while his girlfriend lives here in Northern California.

What I am trying to illustrate with each of these examples that happen to span several generations is that having a long-distance relationship is not necessarily a bad option or a kiss of death to your relationship if you are willing to work at it. Oftentimes, I think, having some distance, especially early in a relationship, can be a good thing. It allows couples time to get to know each other through conversations, ensuring that the physical, sexual side of the relationship doesn't overshadow the psychoemotional part, as often happens.

So if you find yourself in a long-distance relationship with a romantic partner or just a friend, make the effort to include a well-timed and interesting question each Skype/phone call or e-mail to help further develop or maintain your closeness when the miles separate you. Be sure to also use questions from other chapters, especially the "Anniversary" and "Romance and Sex" chapters if your long-distance relationship happens to be a romantic one.

Questions

1. How was your day?
2. What has happened to you of significance since we last talked?
3. How has your life changed since we were last together/lived in the same area?
4. How is your life the same?
5. What do you miss most about us being in the same town?
6. What do you miss most about me?
7. What do you value most about our relationship, even from afar?
8. When will we be together next? (*Having a concrete date for the next time you will be together is important in order to maintain a sense of optimism and hope—a light at the end of the tunnel, so to speak.*)
9. What do we want to do when we are together next?
10. What are you doing right this minute? What are you wearing? Where are you? Are you seated or standing up? Who is with you? (*This provides a mental picture if you are not Skyping or FaceTiming.*)
11. What would I be surprised to learn about you in your new living environment?

12. What would I be surprised to learn about your new college/town?
13. What is school/work like for you?
14. Who have you met that is interesting and/or a potential friend?
15. What activities are you doing that are fun?
16. If you could have me around during one part of your day, which would it be and why?
17. How are people the same/different in that area?
18. Are you experiencing any culture shock?
19. What good restaurants or food have you found?
20. What good stores, vendors, or outdoor markets have you found?
21. When I visit, what do you think I will enjoy most about the area/culture/geography/climate?
22. When I visit, what do you think I will enjoy or notice the most about the people?
23. When I visit, what will be the most different or challenging about the area/culture/geography/climate?
24. When I visit, what will be the most different or challenging about the people?
25. How has living apart stretched your "comfort zone"?
26. How has living apart strengthened our relationship?
27. How has living apart tested our relationship?

NEW PARENTS

Looking back, I don't think I have ever been as tired as when I was working full time and had two young children, one a toddler and one a baby. I was bone tired. I was can't-get-off-the-couch tired. I was a mess.

It took a great therapist and giving myself permission to leave the kids with their dad one night a week to attend a yoga class to come out of it. Therapy and yoga not only saved me, but they saved my marriage too. It's just too easy during those early years of parenting to put yourself and marriage last. And I don't think we, our society, talk about it enough. After I rebounded, I made it one of my missions in life to tell as many young women as I could what those early years of parenting were like for me and how it is imperative, guilt be damned, to carve out time for themselves and their partners.

So this chapter is special to me. It's a relatively short chapter but a critical one. My advice to new parent(s) is simple. Go on a date regularly (and not just when all the stars align perfectly) with your partner or yourself, and ask yourself or each other the questions below. If you just can't swing or afford a date, create an activity such as my coworker and her husband did. Every night before they went to bed, they each wrote down on a piece of paper what they were grateful for in each other from that day (e.g., making dinner, encouraging words, night feeding, etc.). Then they put their statements of gratitude in a paper bag on their nightstands next to their bed. In the morning when they awoke, they would get to read what the other had written. What a great way to start and end each day!

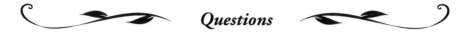

Questions

1. How has my/our life changed since having a child/children?
2. How has my/our life remained the same in spite of having a child/children?
3. In what ways is my/our life better as a result of having a child/children?
4. In what ways is my/our life more difficult as a result of having a child/children?
5. How has motherhood/fatherhood changed you?
6. How has parenthood changed us as a couple?
7. What has been the biggest surprise regarding parenthood?
8. In what ways is being a parent more complicated than you expected?
9. In what ways is being a parent simpler than you expected?
10. What do you enjoy most about being a father/mother?
11. What do you enjoy least about being a father/mother?
12. What help or support do you need?
13. What help or support do we need?
14. What change or adjustments do we need to make?
15. What do you see of yourself or family members reflected in the baby/child?
16. What stage have you enjoy most thus far? Why?
17. What stage have you enjoyed least thus far? Why?
18. What are you looking forward to as a parent?
19. Is parenthood what you expected? How? How not?
20. What advice would you give new parents?

NEW YEAR'S

I have to admit something. I have never known what to do with either New Year's Eve or New Year's Day. Both days expect—no, demand—attention, but I am usually just too worn out from Christmas and all of the family birthdays that surround it to give New Year's Eve and Day their due.

Not that we haven't tried. My husband and I have done the five-course-dinner-with-complimentary-Champagne outing with friends. We once hosted our own black tie affair (or as close as our wardrobe would allow) at home with a pair of our closest friends. With this same group of agreeable friends, we spent a New Year's Eve together in pajamas, playing board games. To be honest, that event was more my style.

But no matter how you choose to ring in the new year, take a moment to reflect on the old year and anticipate the new. So whether you are watching the ball drop in a tuxedo or in your well-worn pajamas, with a flute of Champagne or a mug of hot tea, take the time to make it memorable by having a worthy conversation.

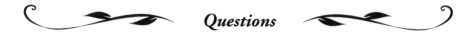 *Questions*

Last Year

1. What was the highlight of last year?
2. What about last year are you eager to leave behind?
3. What surprised you most about last year?
4. What was your biggest lesson from last year?
5. If you could relive one moment from last year, what would it be?
6. If you could have a do-over from last year, what would it be?
7. What relationship of yours deepened the most last year?
8. What relationship improved or began to heal last year?
9. What new hobby or skill did you develop last year?
10. What was your greatest accomplishment last year?
11. What was the biggest risk you took last year?

New Year

1. What are you looking forward to most in the coming year?
2. What is something that was left unfinished last year that you want to complete this year?
3. What relationship would you like to work on or improve this year?
4. What is a past mistake that you want to avoid this year?
5. How do you intend that you and your life will be different a year from now?
6. What risk would you like to take this year?
7. What new hobby or skill would you like to investigate or develop?
8. What do you hope to accomplish by next year?
9. Who is someone you need to reach out to more in the coming year?
10. What needs to happen this year for you to feel satisfied a year from now?
11. What question do you want answered in the coming year?
12. What lesson do you hope to learn this year?

RECONCILIATION

We all experience conflict. It is inevitable. Unless you are living in a cave, far from civilization and totally self-sufficient, conflict is going to be a part of your life. Though conflict often creates anxiety and many of us will do just about anything to avoid it, it is actually a necessary and natural by-product of being human in relationships with other humans. In fact, I would argue that without conflict, we can never really experience personal growth or true and sustainable friendship and intimacy.

I say that not because I am cynical, but because I recognize the need for conflict in order to grow and expand. Conflict allows us to learn more about ourselves and others. When our beliefs, values, and boundaries come into contrast or opposition with someone else's, we are offered the opportunity to question, modify, or recommit to our own. That ongoing process of reviewing what we espouse or hold dear helps to mold us into what we ultimately and hopefully become: wiser.

Another role that conflict has had in my life is that of teacher. Midway into my career, I found myself repeatedly working with colleagues who I perceived as overcontrolling, rigid, and pushy. I kept fretting about it and whined whenever possible that they didn't play fair. Like a schoolchild on the playground, I tried my best to avoid these workplace bullies.

After several years of avoidance behavior (I guess I am a slow learner), I realized that until I stood up to them and dealt with the conflict respectfully and directly, I was destined to continue to have these "teachers" show up in my life. My lesson was clear. Learn to set and communicate boundaries or continue to have conflict, even if it was just internal. I ultimately did just that, and the conflict that I had spent so much time avoiding finally subsided.

I also know from my study of leadership, and group dynamics in particular, that conflict is a normal and necessary stage of any group or team. And I don't mean just in the workplace, but with friends and family too. Taking from Bruce Tuckman's work (Developmental Sequences in Small Groups), people who spend significant and ongoing time together are likely to experience four distinct, linear, and at the same time fluid stages if they allow and deal with conflict constructively. Those stages are "forming," "storming," "norming," and "performing." Unless a group of people or team experiences the storming phase that comes with being real with each other, they will not be able to enjoy the productive and deeply satisfying performing stage that follows.

So when I was asked recently by one of my staff members to bear witness and facilitate a reconciliation process between her and someone she supervised (they also knew each other socially), I jumped at the chance. I was especially eager to participate when I reviewed the steps and questions that each was to answer. In my role as witness and facilitator, I helped them keep on track and use "I statements" and shared my insight as we proceeded. It was truly an honor to watch these two women engage in a process that led toward deeper understanding and appreciation for the other. Did their relationship immediately transform and become perfect and devoid of any problems? No. But in my experience, reconciliation takes time and requires continued patience and commitment. They did, however, create an open line of communication that continues to this day. Before you begin the more involved reconciliation process, you may want to start by asking the question I often use with someone with whom I feel out of sync. It is simple but nonthreatening and usually very effective.

"Are we OK?"

In my experience, this question leads to either a "Yes, why do you ask" or a "No. I have been feeling kind of tense or awkward with you..." response. Either comment opens the doors for a conversation about the relationship and an opportunity to gain mutual understanding, clarity, and the chance to apologize if the occasion calls for it. Even if the apology is something like, "I am sorry if you misunderstood my comments or motives and this has caused you distress. That was not my intent. Let me clarify...," it will be appreciated.

If, however, you sense the need for a more in-depth and structured process for reconciliation, try the steps (adopted and modified from JoAnna Macey's The Work That Reconnects) below. You can ask each question either casually and separately or more formally, as I did with my two employees. If you choose the latter, be sure to ask all involved if they are open and agreeable to the process. Also, it is only fair to provide the questions to all in advance so everyone participating has equal time to consider and prepare for his or her responses.

Questions

1. What aspects (present or past) are you grateful for in your friendship, relationship, and/or this situation (positive moments or experiences)?
2. What is the root pain and what need is not being met or honored? What do you care deeply about related to this situation or friendship?
3. How would this situation look and feel different from another perspective other than your own? Can you try and see this situation from the other's lens?
4. What are the next steps toward healing, forgiveness, and planting new seeds?

ROMANCE AND SEX

Who doesn't need more romance and sex in his or her life? After being married for thirty-five years, I certainly could use more. But in hindsight, and if I am honest with myself, I could have used more romance and sex during most stages of my life. I am absolutely certain my husband would say the same. It is just too easy to place both romance and sex to the bottom of the priority list.

So my advice is make time for both. Even schedule it if necessary. I know that flies in the face of spontaneity, but in our busy and calendared lives, sometimes setting aside time for both romance and sex is the only way we give ourselves permission to please ourselves and our partners in this special way. And remember that romance enhances sex and vice versa, so try to include both whenever possible.

Here is an example. When our children were younger, my husband and I agreed to take turns planning a romantic getaway. In the fall, he was responsible for identifying a location, booking the accommodations, and arranging the childcare (usually my parents). I was responsible for the spring trip. In each case, the person planning kept the location a secret and told the other only what to bring in terms of appropriate clothing. During those megahectic years, those weekend trips were essential to keeping our romantic and sexual embers glowing.

If finances or lack of available babysitters (should you have children) prohibit this luxury, start simple. My husband and I love walks in the park. Establish a date night each week, or month, for that matter. It will also go a long way to helping you connect or stay connected with your partner. And whether you are walking in the park or having a great meal out, remember to discuss romance and sex themselves. I am no expert in either subject, but I can't help but think that having an honest and tender conversation about both romance and sex is a great starting pointing for initiating or improving these aspects of your life and relationship.

 *Questions*

Romance

1. What does romance mean to you?
2. What is the most romantic thing I have ever done for you?
3. What is the most romantic thing I could do for you?
4. What romantic gesture have you always longed for?
5. If you could create your most romantic day, what would it include?
6. If you could create your most romantic evening, what would it include?
7. If you could create your most romantic weekend, what would it include?
8. What is the most romantic book you have ever read? Why?
9. What is the most romantic movie you have ever seen? Why? (*Books and movies are excellent sources of inspiration and ideas related to romance and sex.*)
10. What simple gestures or activities feel romantic to you?
11. What isn't romantic to you?
12. What is something you could do right this minute that would be considered romantic to your partner?
13. If you had only fifteen minutes to plan something romantic for your partner, what would it be?
14. If you had a full day to plan something romantic for your partner, what would it be?

Sex

1. What does sex mean to you?
2. What animal represents your sexuality and why?
3. What are your boundaries—things you are willing and not willing to do sexually?
4. What are some unexplored activities that you would like to try?
5. What do I need to know about you sexually?
6. What are some turn-ons?
7. What are some turnoffs?
8. What sexual fantasies do you have?
9. What sexual fantasies do you have that you would like to act out?
10. What clothes, activities, or settings make you feel most sexual?
11. Where and when do you feel most sexual?
12. Where and when do you feel least sexual?
13. What parts of your body respond well to touch?
14. What parts of your body do you feel awkward about or dislike to have touched?

SEEKING THE SPIRITUAL

I am a big fan of Oprah's Super Soul Sunday. I think I have watched every episode. At the conclusion of each show, Oprah will ask her guests, among other things, for their definition of and the difference between spirituality and religion. What I gleaned from these experts is that religion is a set of shared and agreed-upon rules, rituals, and beliefs that give people's faith a shape, context, and purpose. Religion attempts to explain the unexplainable and give it meaning. Spirituality, on the other hand, is the internal and direct connection with the divine and all other things, living and nonliving, of this world and not of this world. Spirituality, to my way of thinking, is how we think about, interact with, and manifest the divine through love.

As you might suspect, I have always been drawn to questions of a spiritual nature. More so than religious ones. I think we all are spiritually inquisitive, and from a young age, if we are given the encouragement, validation, and space to do so. There is just too much that is unknown and so much about which to wonder and speculate for us not to ponder. And I don't think there is one definitive or right answer to most of these questions, no matter what some religious leaders and devotees may have us believe.

So if no one person or faith has all the answers, as is my opinion, then this permits each of us a seat at the spiritual table to share equally our opinions, experiences, and beliefs related to the origin, meaning, and ultimate outcome of life. What a banquet this can be! I hope the questions below assist you in this potential feast of contemplation and conversation. I have one request though. Please don't forget the children during this taste testing of ideas. Often they have insight that is simple, awe inspiring, and not yet tainted or jaded by dogma. Bon appetit!

Questions

1. Where do you think we come from?
2. Where do you think we will go upon death?
3. What are your beliefs regarding the origin of life?
4. What are your beliefs regarding the inherent nature of humankind?
5. In what ways, if any, do you think we are connected to those who have passed on and those who have yet to come?
6. What is the difference between being religious and being spiritual?
7. Can you be spiritual without believing in the divine? Explain.
8. Where and when do you feel most connected to the divine?
9. Who have been your spiritual teachers or mentors? What did they teach or model for you?
10. Do we humans need organized religion? Why or why not?
11. Do you believe in reincarnation? Why or why not?
12. What is our purpose in living?
13. Do you believe in souls and, if so, who or what on earth possesses one?
14. In what ways, if any, are we humans and nonhumans linked?
15. If you could have one spiritual question answered by the divine, what would it be?
16. When, if ever, have you felt touched by the divine?
17. When, if ever, have you needed the touch of the divine most?

SIBLING GATHERINGS

When my parents died within two-and-a-half years of each other over a decade ago, the glue between my brothers and me, and our respective families, began to erode. To be fair, my brothers and I live two states apart, and at the time of my mother's death, our children were also coming to an age of adolescence and early adulthood that meant their interests and obligations were beginning to take them in different directions anyway. But prior to losing my parents, I was accustomed to seeing my siblings, and nieces and nephews, several times a year, including many holidays. That certainly wasn't the case afterward. Seeing them once a year, if that, became the new norm.

Though I could intellectually rationalize it initially, losing connection with my brothers after losing my parents ultimately felt like loss heaped on top of more loss. I was devastated. And I'm guessing our family is not unique. As I talk with friends about this postparent phenomenon, many share their own sadness and frustration about siblings who were once close but now are seemingly scattered to the wind.

I realize that for some families, parents are the only thing their children have in common. Some families were dysfunctional before the matriarch and patriarch died, and can become even more so afterward. But that was not the case in my family. We were just busy with our respective lives, and our parents, who lived in my town, were no longer the magnets that pulled them to me and mine.

At first, I felt enormous grief, then anger, followed by resentment. I'm fairly sure I whined a lot to my brothers about why they didn't call or visit or both more often. I also complained that as the youngest and only girl in the family, it should not be assumed or expected that I plan all of the get-togethers or come to Seattle, where they lived. I would not recommend the nagging or self-pity approach as a way to attract or draw people to you. It certainly did not work for me.

What did work is when I suggested that instead of trying to organize gatherings that included everyone (which is nearly impossible given that the cousins now live in five different states), we should focus on a sibling-only gathering. So nearly six years ago, my brothers and I committed to one extended weekend each winter to being together—just the three of us. And to avoid any one sibling feeling put upon, we alternate who plans and arranges the weekend. Together, we have gone to Lake Tahoe, Central Oregon, and Orcas Island, to name a few.

I am happy to report that Sibling Weekend has been a great success. Not only do we spend time in beautiful places, doing fun things (usually hiking and great food are involved), but we spend time having meaningful conversations.

Please know, though, reunions and conversations with your siblings need not and should not wait until the death of your parents or once you reach middle age. Instead start the practice early and, in so doing, make meaningful conversations the norm, not the exception. This habit will also serve to demonstrate to the next generation how staying in touch with a sister or brother can include more than a text or Facebook message.

If you don't know how to begin, use the question I asked my brothers on our first weekend together. I asked it while we drove three hundred miles to Yosemite National Park, and it took nearly the entire distance for the three of us to take turns answering it: What is your childhood story? Or, what was your childhood like?

This is a wonderful place to start, primarily because many of us are under the illusion that we had the same parents and the same childhood. Nothing could be further from the truth. Depending on your birth order, gender, sexual orientation, what was happening in your parents' marriage, or their financial well-being, children can have significantly different experiences within the same family. So if possible, start with this question and be open to hearing that all was not what it seemed among you and your siblings.

The following are some additional questions.

Questions

1. What positive characteristics do you have in common with Dad?
2. What positive characteristics do you have in common with Mom?
3. What negative characteristics do you have from each parent?
4. What characteristics do you have in common with each of us siblings?
5. What is something that we siblings would be surprised to learn about you?
6. What are some of your happiest memories spent with our family?
7. What are some of the saddest or most challenging moments spent with our family?
8. In what way did our family perceive you correctly growing up?
9. In what way did our family misperceive you? *(This is a sensitive question and should be asked only after trust has been established, but it is an important and empowering question, as it gives us each an opportunity to dispel or correct myths about ourselves.)*
10. What are you most proud of related to our family?
11. What would you change about our family if you could? *(Again, wait until trust is established before you ask this one.)*
12. What would the neighbors, family friends, and community be surprised to learn about our family?
13. What are your favorite family traditions?
14. What were your favorite family holidays?
15. What were your favorite family vacations?
16. If your childhood was to become a movie, what would the title be and why?
17. If your childhood was to become a movie, which actor or actress would you want to play each sibling and why?
18. What are some family memories that still make you laugh?
19. What are some family memories that still make you sad or angry?
20. What did you learn most from each sibling?
21. What role did each sibling play in your life?
22. What did you learn of most value from each parent?
23. What did you learn of most value from your family as a whole?

THANKSGIVING

I WROTE THIS ARTICLE FOR NORTH STATE PARENT *MAGAZINE, THE NOVEMBER 2013 EDITION.*

I don't know about you, but once the candles are blown out, the leftovers are safely in the fridge, and I have changed into sweat pants (the expandable type), I tend to experience a little Thanksgiving letdown. My belly is full, but often my soul is not. I become a little melancholy and wonder, "Is that all there is?" Or at least I used to. Now I have no excuse for having a less than fulfilling Thanksgiving, or any holiday or major event, for that matter. The reason for the shift is because I wrote a book titled Life Talks—A Guide to Bringing Back Conversation, which addressed the need we all have to connect in a meaningful way with others, especially our family and friends.

If you don't know where to start in terms of creating new traditions and building memories, you are not alone. I find that many people are a little reticent to tackle a full-blown "team builder" with unsuspecting family members and friends.

My answer is, start with Thanksgiving. As I state in Life Talks, "If you are wondering how you are going to introduce conversation starters to your friends and family members because you fear the reaction you might get, then Thanksgiving is the perfect holiday on which to begin. There is, after all, a directive implicit in the word Thanksgiving: give thanks."

Here is how you can start this new tradition. Call people to dinner, and as you do, explain that you are initiating a new tradition. Have everyone gather around the table and ask everyone to hold hands (optional) while each person shares at least one thing that he or she is thankful for. Even the youngest members should be encouraged to participate. They may need a little prompting, but you will be surprised by what they may say.

If that feels too basic or your family already participates in gratitude sharing, I suggest you try another activity, which is also in the book and is one that my mother started years ago. She would make place cards for the table with our names on them and ask the grandkids to randomly place them around the table. When you sat in your assigned seat, my mother would direct us to look inside the folded place card, where we would find a question that we had to answer sometime before the meal concluded. Her questions tended to be whimsical and fun and included ones such as "If you could meet a famous person...," "If you had unlimited money...," or "If you could create any kind of theme park...."

A variation of this theme is to select questions from the Life Talks "Thanksgiving" chapter or from other chapters of the book. Examples from the "Family Reunion" chapter: "What superhero do you most identify with?" and "What are three things this group would be surprised to learn about your?" From the "Long Car Rides" chapter: "What is one thing you appreciate about the family?" and "What is something you are really good at doing?"

Print the questions out and place them in a basket, bag, or hat. As family members arrive, have them pick a question from the grab bag and explain that they will need to answer the question during dinner. By distributing the questions early, you provide the folks that are more introverted a chance to think about their response ahead of time. You can also allow trading to occur, so if someone is absolutely puzzled by the question he or she gets, he or she can swap it with someone else.

What is great about the use of questions is that there is an unlimited supply of them (If you run out of ideas, ask others for ideas) and no minimum number is required to participate. Whether you are a small family of two or a large one, the benefit is the same: creating opportunities to really connect in both fun and meaningful ways.

I wrote Life Talks so that none of us has to experience another holiday or major life event where we leave the table feeling empty. Happy holidays!

 *Questions*

1. If you could spend a day with a famous person, who would it be, and what questions would you ask them?
2. You have an appointment with a medium and you have the opportunity to talk with a friend or family member who has passed over. Who would you choose to talk to, and what would you ask them?
3. Which event in history would you have liked to have been present at and why?
4. What is one thing that no one here knows about you?
5. Which event in the future would you like to be present at and why?

6. What is one talent you possess that you would not want to live without?
7. What continues to surprise you about life?
8. What continues to surprise you about yourself?
9. You have been given unlimited resources to create a business. What would it be?
10. You have been given one million dollars and the directive to donate it to worthy causes that don't benefit you or your family. How would you spend the money?
11. If you could create a form of transportation not yet developed, what would it be?
12. If you had the ability to solve a significant conflict in the world or cure a major disease, what would you solve or cure?
13. What talent do you currently possess but have not fully developed?
14. What five things remain on your bucket list?
15. If you knew that you had five years left to live, how would your life stay the same and how would it change?
16. You have been given unlimited resources to create a totally new and unique theme park. What would it be?

VACATIONS

What better way to end this book than with a discussion about my favorite topic and pastime, vacations? Vacations are what I do best. My best memories in life, and I'm not kidding, are almost all associated with traveling with either my family of origin or now with my husband and children and close friends.

While growing up, most of my family vacations included camping with intermittent stops at roadside motels. Picking the right motel was fraught with excitement and anxiety. We alternated between eagerness to find just the right place and fear that once we found it, it would be too expensive or too popular, as indicated by a no-vacancy sign. The right place to my mother was a room with air conditioning and a spotless bathroom. My brothers and I cared about one thing only: Did it have a pool? We didn't even care if the pool was green with algae or if pollywogs swam with us. If it was wet, we were content.

During my formative years, my parents, brothers, and I visited nearly every major national park in the western United States. Sometimes we traveled alone, but other times we traveled with family friends. Traveling with other families was optimal, as it increased the chances that we had additional playmates, which in turn helped minimize in-family squabbles.

During these camping excursions, even helping my mother with what were usually mundane chores, such as fetching water and washing dishes, became exotic and fun. Plus, getting dirty was not only allowed but encouraged. It doesn't get any better than that, or at least I didn't think so until later in my life.

During my early to midtwenties, I discovered a new kind of vacation, the worldly kind. While in my first year of grad school, I saved up enough money by working two and sometimes three jobs to travel to Europe with a good friend the following summer. With entirely too much luggage and one pack of cigarettes between us (we thought it would make us appear more sophisticated), we set out to see what Europe had to offer. After two months, seven countries, and a half-dozen cigarettes each (being sophisticated isn't always what it is cracked up to be), we returned home new women. Not only were we more confident after negotiating new cultures, currencies, and languages, we also knew that this was only the beginning. Our appetites had been whetted and we were eager to see even more of the world.

So it is not surprising that my husband and I have offered our children opportunities for both varieties of vacations, camping and cross-cultural. Together, we have crisscrossed the United States (often with a tent trailer) and ventured overseas. And fortunately for me, my job has taken me all over the world, including Egypt, India, Eastern Europe, Sweden, South and Central America, Japan, and South Korea.

And though I feel strongly that everyone needs to leave his or her own country at least once (if not more) to expand his or her world view, a vacation does not have to cost lots of money or require passports. Vacations can be spending a weekend camping in your backyard or a week exploring your local area. The point of a vacation is, after all, to spend uninterrupted time and to reconnect with yourself, family, and friends. Vacations are also meant to recharge your batteries and preferably learn something new. I wholeheartedly believe spending time vacationing with my family is one of the most important traditions we practice!

So in that spirit, let me assist you and your band of merry travelers by providing some questions to help you plan, experience, and process your next vacation.

Please note: When answering the prevacation questions, give yourself adequate time in advance so that if modifications to your plans or itinerary need to be made, you have ample time to do so. And if not traveling solo, try to include as many of the members going on the trip as possible when discussing trip locales, goals, and expectations.

 *Questions*

Before the Vacation

1. Given the budget and time available, where would you like to go for vacation? *(when my brothers and I got into our teens, our parents began to include us in the decision making regarding our summer vacations, which I very much appreciated.)*

2. Given the location and budget, what activities or places are important for you to do and see?

3. What will make this vacation a success for you? *(I learned early on that my husband and children liked to sleep in on vacation and participate in a limited number of activities each day. They are also more spontaneous than I, so we had to learn to adapt to each other. Answering this question ahead of time helped us to do that.)*

4. What is the amount each child will receive for spending money on souvenirs? *(We told our children early in the vacation how much they could spend on souvenirs, and then it was their choice how and when to spend it.)*

5. What clothing, accessories, equipment, and supplies are necessary for the vacation?

6. What books or online resources would help plan or prepare for the vacation?

7. What accommodations or reservations need to be made in advance?

8. What are your transportation options?

9. Is your itinerary reasonable? Have you checked with everyone vacationing with you for their input and opinions?

10. What is your goal or intention for the vacation? Have you planned the vacation in such a way that you are likely to meet your and others' goals?

During the Vacation

1. How is everyone doing (general check-in)?

2. How is the pace of the vacation so far?

3. So far, what have you enjoyed doing the most?

4. What has met or exceeded your expectations?

5. What has fallen short or not met your expectations?

6. What adjustment or changes, if any, need to be made to the itinerary to make the vacation more enjoyable or fun for all?

7. What has surprised you?

8.   What have you learned?
9.   What is left that you want to do or accomplish?
10.   How much money or resources do we have left to work with?

After the Vacation

1.   What was most enjoyable about the vacation?
2.   What stretched your comfort zone the most?
3.   What were some of the lessons you learned on this vacation?
4.   How did you surprise yourself *(in a good way)*?
5.   What was the riskiest thing you did?
6.   What are you most grateful for regarding the vacation?
7.   Who do we need to thank for the vacation?
8.   If we had a chance to do this vacation over again, what would we do the same and what would we do differently?
9.   What were the high and low points of the vacation?
10.   What is our next vacation going to be and what have we learned from this vacation that we can apply to the next?

EPILOGUE:
LIFE TALKS—THE CONVERSATIONS CONTINUE

As with many of my life's decisions, I didn't necessarily know what I was getting myself into when I first decided to write a book titled Life Talks—A Guide to Bringing Back Conversation, nor where it was going to take me, but I took the plunge and hoped for the best. In December of 2012, I began a journey I could never have imagined. It was truly a leap of faith, and though the book is hardly a best seller (yet) and I have not met Oprah (yet)—both goals of mine when I started out—it has been quite the adventure and a learning experience nonetheless. As it turns out, my decision was a good one, but not necessarily for the reasons I had anticipated.

For instance, writing Life Talks provided me an opportunity to gain knowledge and learn skills that, had I not written the book, I never would have acquired, or needed to, for that matter. I learned—with a lot of support and guidance from others—how to self-publish, build a website and Facebook page, and market the book and myself.

It also became apparent early in this process that I needed to "walk my talk." In both Life Talks—A Guide to Bringing Back Conversation and Life Talks—The Conversations Continue, I challenge you, the readers, to take a risk and create opportunities to have more meaningful conversations. Ironically, I too had to learn to make connections in new ways, often with strangers, and in new venues, such as farmers' markets, book fairs, book signings, and PTA parents' nights. Let's just say, that never before had I ever presented to a group of parents at a skating rink while their children were busy skating to music from One Direction! I also learned how to write a magazine article with very little lead time (twenty-four hours) and how to be interviewed on the radio, but that is another story and another unanticipated set of skills.

At first, I was self-conscious, awkward, and lacked confidence, particularly

111

when describing and talking about my book and, by extension, myself. I felt a bit presumptuous telling people that I had written a book or having others refer to me as an author. For the first six months, my self-perception hadn't caught up with my new reality: that I am in fact an author and that I have something important to say!

Yet that is precisely what I want you to do: take a risk and reach out to others. Life Talks—A Guide to Bringing Back Conversation and now Life Talks—The Conversations Continue encourage and empower readers to create traditions and start conversations with their partners, children, parents, coworkers, and friends and, in so doing, to create deeper and more meaningful relationships. The message throughout both books is that each of us—as authors of our own lives—has something important to say and that we just need the time, opportunity, and safe spaces to say it.

If, after reading either book, you find yourself initiating and implementing one or more of my suggested activities, congratulations! You made a decision, took a risk, and hopefully the outcome gives you the courage to try another one or improvise and create your own. You may already come from a family and work environment that value these kinds of activities and are just looking for new ideas. If that is the case, you are blessed. Keep up the good work! If, on the other hand, you try one and it falls flat, don't be discouraged.

Furthermore, if at first you find yourself feeling self-conscious, awkward, and presumptuous while leading one of the team builders or icebreakers in this book, you are in good company! After all, that is what implementing change does for us. It places us firmly outside our comfort zones and onto a new path or direction that forces us to stretch and expand. Often, we must acquire new skills and hone old ones. Seldom is there not risk involved. And we must begin to see ourselves, our relationships, and our communities in a new light.

Moreover, new habits take time. And it takes time and repetition before these new traditions and ways of connecting will begin to feel normal and natural to you and your family, friends, and colleagues. Be patient with yourself and others as you create this new way of being together.

The important thing, though, is that you keep trying. We humans need to continue to find ways to connect with each other in fun and rewarding ways, especially during this era of technology. In fact, one of the most common remarks I have received when discussing my book is how timely and important this topic is given our growing dependency on social media for our connections and communication. There seems to be a growing realization and concern, regardless of age and generation, that as we evolve our technological skills and applications, we may inadvertently be decreasing our ability to communicate face to face. Life Talks—A Guide to Bringing Back Conversation and Life Talks—The Conversations Continue are my small effort in making sure that doesn't happen.

Write your additional questions here!

Write your additional questions here!

ABOUT THE AUTHOR

Peggy is a retired community college administrator who lives with her husband and two dogs in both Northern California and Central Oregon. She is the author of Life Talks—A Guide to Bringing Back Conversation.

Contact
lifetalksbook@gmail.com

Website
www.lifetalksbook.com

Facebook
www.facebook.com/lifetalksbook

Made in the USA
Middletown, DE
12 July 2019